PALM SPRINGS MADE EASY

Andy Herbach
Karl Raaum

Made Easy Travel Guides

www.madeeasytravelguides.com

PALM SPRINGS MADE EASY
Andy Herbach and Karl Raaum
Fourth edition © 2023
ISBN: 9798853990593
Acknowledgments
Editor: Marian Modesta Olson
Thanks to our contributors: Jim Phillips, Erin Raaum, and Donn Walker
All photos from Karl Raaum, Shutterstock, Wikimedia Images, and Pixabay

ABOUT THE AUTHORS

Andy Herbach is the author of the *Eating & Drinking* series of menu translators and restaurant guides, including *Eating & Drinking in Paris, Eating & Drinking in Italy, Eating & Drinking in Spain and Portugal, Eating & Drinking in Germany,* and *Eating & Drinking in Latin America*. He is also the author of several travel guides, including *Paris Walks, The Next Time I See Paris, Paris Made Easy, Europe Made Easy, Amsterdam Made Easy, Berlin Made Easy, Barcelona Made Easy, Madrid Made Easy, Oslo Made Easy, Nice and the French Riviera Made Easy, Provence Made Easy, Wales Made Easy, The Amazing California Desert, Palm Springs Made Easy, San Diego Made Easy,* and *Southern California Made Easy*. **Karl Raaum** has contributed to all of the *Made Easy* travel guides and is the co-author of *The Next Time I See Paris, Palm Springs Made Easy, Southern California Made Easy, San Diego Made Easy*, and *The Amazing California Desert*. The authors reside in Palm Springs, California, USA.

You can e-mail corrections, additions, and comments to eatndrink@aol.com or through www.madeeasytravelguides.com.

TABLE OF CONTENTS

1. Introduction   7

2. Palm Springs and the Coachella Valley   9

3. Joshua Tree National Park and the Hi-Desert   60

4. Excursions   81
   Cabazon   82
   Salton Sea   83
   Idyllwild   87
   Big Bear   90

5. Sleeping & Eating   91
   Sleeping   91
   Eating   101

6. Shopping   111

7. Planning Your Trip/Practical Matters   114

8. Index   117

MAPS

California   8
Coachella Valley   10
Palm Springs Sights   14
Mid-Century Modern Sights   19
Coachella Valley Casinos   34
Pools   37
Hiking   45
Golfing   52
Joshua Tree National Park   64-65
Hi-Desert   71
Salton Sea   85
Sleeping   93
Eating   102
Shopping   111

4

Escape the summer heat by floating in a pool!

Take a tour of the iconic windmills that dot the valley.

Hike the incredible Joshua Tree National Park.

5

Play a round of golf on one of the best courses in the country.

Ride the Aerial Tramway, the world's largest rotating tram car.

Visit the Living Desert Zoo and Gardens in Palm Desert.

REVIEWS OF OUR TRAVEL GUIDES

•

"..an opinionated little compendium."
Eating & Drinking in Paris
~ New York Times

"Everything you need to devour Paris on the quick."
Best of Paris
~ Chicago Tribune

"an elegant, small guide..."
Eating & Drinking in Italy
~ Minneapolis Star Tribune

"Makes dining easy and enjoyable."
Eating & Drinking in Spain
~ Toronto Sun

"Guide illuminates the City of Light."
Wining & Dining in Paris
~ Newsday

"This handy pocket guide is all you need..."
Paris Made Easy
~ France Magazine

"Small enough for discreet use..."
Eating & Drinking in Paris
~ USA Today

"It's written as if a friend were talking to you."
Eating & Drinking in Italy
~ Celebrity Chef Tyler Florence

1. INTRODUCTION

Palm Springs has something for everyone. If you love nature, there are spectacular hiking trails to explore, and the breathtaking Aerial Tramway. If art is your passion, take in the Palm Springs Art Museum, or the Uptown District's galleries.

How about architecture? After all, you'll be in the heart of Mid-Century Modern and Spanish Revival. And when you need to refuel, take your pick from the many friendly (and festive) restaurants and bars all over downtown and throughout the Coachella Valley.

From the stark beauty of Joshua Tree National Park to exciting nightlife and resorts—including insider tips on cafes, restaurants, and shops—this concise little pocket guide will help you plan your trip with confidence. However short your stay, it's all you'll need to make your visit enjoyable, memorable—and easy!

THINGS CHANGE!
Phone numbers, prices, addresses, and quality of food all change. It would be wise to check websites for updated information before your visit. It's advisable to book online for entrance to many of the most popular sights. Some even allow you to schedule your visit for a specific entry time.

2. Palm Springs and the Coachella Valley

- Aerial Tramway
- Palm Springs Art Museum
- Palm Springs Air Museum
- Living Desert Zoo and Gardens
- Mid-Century Modern Architecture
- Moorten Botanical Garden and Cactarium
- Sunnylands
- Windmill Tours
- *Forever Marilyn*
- Modernism Museum
- Village Green Heritage Center
- Agua Caliente Cultural Museum/ Agua Caliente Cultural Plaza
- Elvis Honeymoon Hideaway
- Arenas Road and the LGBTQ+ Scene
- Museum of Ancient Wonders (MoAW)
- Casinos
- Pools
- The Hollywood Connection/Homes of the Stars
- Hiking
- Golfing/Tennis
- Festivals/Events
- Coachella Valley Preserve
- Date Farm
- Desert Hot Springs

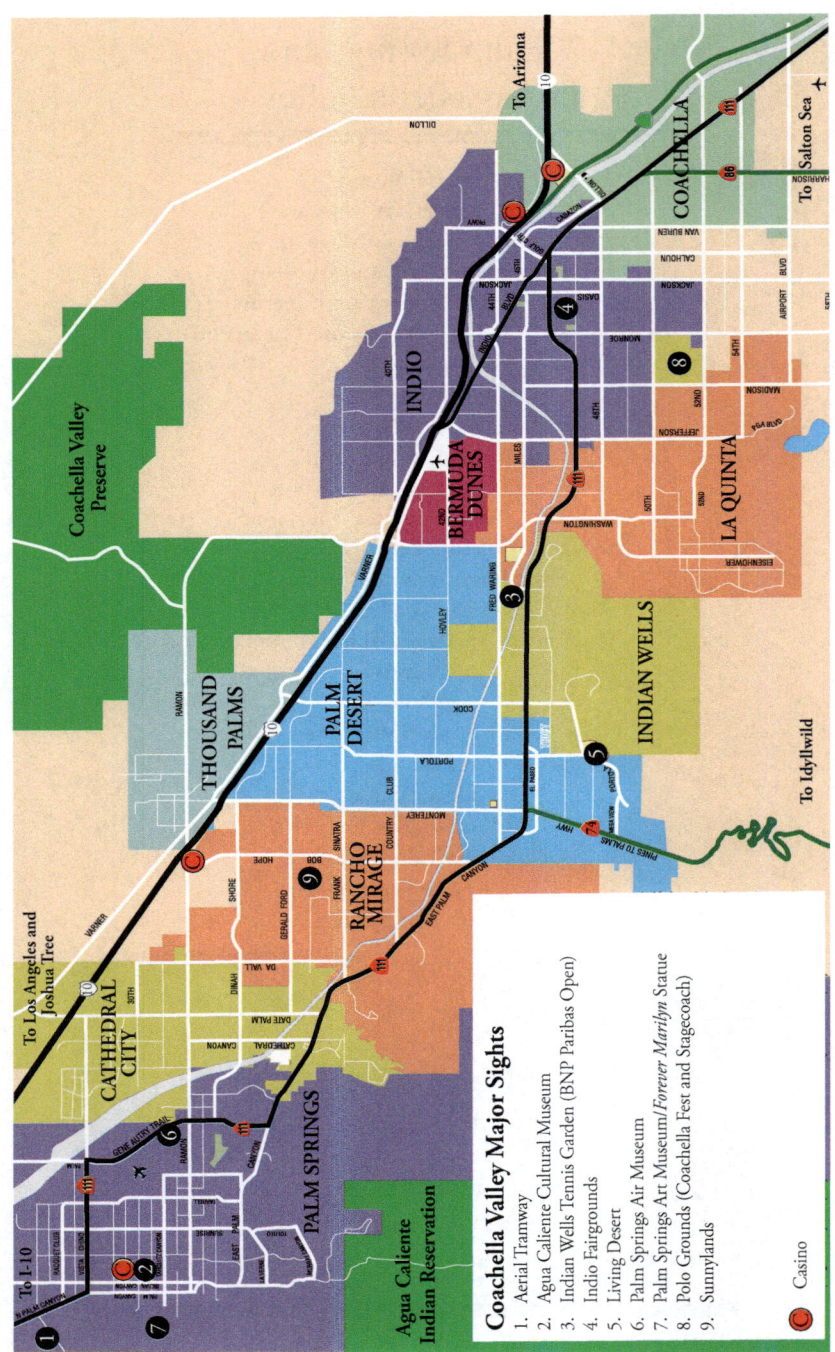

AERIAL TRAMWAY
The Palm Springs Aerial Tramway is the world's largest rotating tram car. Enjoy the breathtaking cliffs of Chino Canyon as you travel 2.5 miles (4 km) up the mountain. The 10-minute ride provides a spectacular view of the Coachella Valley. During your ride, you'll hear about the building of the tram, the different climates, and the surrounding landscape.

At the end of your ride, you'll be at an elevation of 8,516 feet (2,595 meters), in **Mt. San Jacinto State Park**. Once you reach the Mountain Station you can visit the natural history museum, two theaters telling the story of the tram, a gift shop, and two restaurants. Take in the views from the Lookout Lounge while you have a cocktail, eat at the casual Pines Café, or dine at the Peaks Restaurant. From the station, you have access to over 50 miles (80 km) of hiking trails. In the winter, desert visitors and residents can play in the snow and cross-country ski.

Francis Crocker was an engineer who lived in nearby Banning. In 1935, he came up with a plan to connect the desert to the mountains so that people could get away from the oppressive heat in the summer. The impressive project was completed in 1963.

Temperatures average 40°F (5°C) cooler at Mountain Station than in the towns of the Coachella Valley. *Info*: 1 Tram Way Rd., Palm Springs. Tel. 888/515-8726. Open daily Mon-Fri 10am-9:30pm (last tram up 8pm), Sat, Sun, and holidays 8am-9:30pm (last tram up 8pm). Admission: $30.95, ages 3-10 $18.95, over 65 $28.95. www.pstramway.com.

At the bottom of the Tram Road is the **Palm Springs Visitor Center**, housed in a 1956 gas station. This mid-century modern structure features an impressive angular roofline, and was designed by Albert Frey and Robson Chambers. It's often the first thing that visitors see when arriving to the city. *Info*: 2901 N. Palm Canyon Dr. (at Tram Way Rd.), Palm Springs. Tel. 800/347-7746 or 760/778-8418. Open daily 10am-5pm. Admission: Free. www.visitpalmsprings.com.

Right next to the visitor center is the **Palm Springs Welcome Sign**, the perfect photo op with the mountain backdrop.

PALM SPRINGS/COACHELLA VALLEY

PALM SPRINGS ART MUSEUM

Located in the heart of downtown Palm Springs, the **Palm Springs Art Museum** was designed in 1974 by renowned mid-century modern architect E. Stewart Williams.

For a city the size of Palm Springs, the museum's permanent collection of contemporary art—housed in 28 galleries and two sculpture gardens—is quite impressive, including works by Calder, Chagall, Lichtenstein, Picasso, and Warhol. Previously known as the Palm Springs Desert Museum, it also offers a significant collection of Western art, and Native American artifacts. In addition, several temporary exhibitions are offered throughout the year, and the Annenberg Theater stages musical and theatrical performances. The museum also has a store, and a bistro/wine bar. The **Aluminaire House** is being reconstructed next to the museum. It's considered a masterpiece of modernist design. *Info*: 101 N. Museum Dr., Palm Springs. Tel. 760/322-4800. Open Thu noon-8pm, Fri-Sun 10am-5pm. Closed Mon, Tue, and Wed. Admission: $16. Admission is free on Thu from 5pm-8pm, under 18 free. www.psmuseum.org.

Some of the permanent collection is housed at a branch in nearby Palm Desert. Opened in 2012, it's home to the **Faye Sarkowsky Sculpture Garden**, and features 14 sculptures on four acres of desert landscape. *Info*: 72-567 Highway 111. Tel. 760/322-4800. Open daily sunrise to sunset. Admission: Free. www.psmuseum.org/visit/palm-desert.

14 PALM SPRINGS MADE EASY

Palm Springs Sights
1. Aerial Tramway/
   Palm Springs Visitor Center
2. Agua Caliente Cultural Museum
3. Architecture Design Center
4. Elvis Honeymoon Hideaway
5. Moorten Botanical Garden
6. Palm Springs Air Museum
7. Palm Springs Art Museum/
   Forever Marilyn statue
8. Arenas Road
   (LGBTQ bars and nightlife)
9. Movie Colony
10. Old Las Palmas/Vista Las Palmas
11. Village Green Heritage Center

PALM SPRINGS/COACHELLA VALLEY 15

The iconic **Architectural Design Center** in downtown Palm Springs houses a collection of architectural drawings, models, and photographs. Originally designed for the Santa Fe Savings & Loan Association by renowned mid-century modern architect E. Stewart Williams—who also designed the Palm Springs Art Museum—the bank's huge vault now serves as the museum's gift shop! Walking tours, many featuring mid-century modern architecture, can be booked through www.psmuseum.org. *Info*: 300 S. Palm Canyon Dr., Palm Springs. Tel. 760/423-5260. Open Thu noon-8pm, Fri-Sun 10am-5pm. Closed Mon, Tue, and Wed. Admission: $5.

Nestled into the landscape high above the Palm Springs Art Museum, the **Frey House II**, completed in 1964, is the former home of architect Albert Frey, who integrated the site's hillside environment—including a huge boulder—into the home's glass-walled, steel-frame design. Managed  by The Architectural Design Center, the house rightly deserves its reputation as one of the finest examples of modernism in Palm Springs. Tours are offered by special request only or during Modernism Week. *Info*: 686 Palisades Dr., Palm Springs. www.psmuseum.org/visit/frey-house. Reservations through www.moderntour.com. Admission: From $200.

PALM SPRINGS AIR MUSEUM

Dedicated to the history, restoration, and preservation of military aircraft, the Palm Springs Air Museum, located near the Palm Springs International Airport, has one of the world's largest collections of WWII fighters and bombers, in addition to Korean War and Vietnam War aircraft. Much of the museum's collection is housed in three climate-controlled hangars (and most of the planes still fly!). Docents, many of them veterans, guide you through American military history. The Buddy Rodgers Theater shows documentaries about aviation in the military. And ask about activities for the kids! *Info*: 745 N. Gene Autry Trail. Tel. 760/778-6262. Open daily 10am-5pm. Admission: $23, veterans and 65 and over $21. Free: Under age 13, and active military (and their immediate families) with identification. www.palmspringsairmuseum.org.

PALM SPRINGS/COACHELLA VALLEY 17

LIVING DESERT ZOO AND GARDENS
Showcasing exotic flora and fauna from around the world, the Living Desert Zoo and Gardens in Palm Desert will satisfy the intrepid adventurer, plant enthusiast, and animal lover in all of us! General admission to the 1200-acre park will provide hours of exploring—including the nature preserve and paved hiking trails—surrounded by extraordinary desert plants of all shapes and sizes. The four-acre Rhino Savanna is now open and home to 12 African species.

Get there early, and the kids can help feed the giraffes (9am-11am daily, additional $8). Ride the carousel, featuring endangered species. And if you love butterflies and hummingbirds, visit the Winged Wonders Pavilion. Then there's a petting zoo ... a wildlife show ... a reptile show ... private, guided tours ... and much more. Visit their website for additional information, events, and prices. *Info*: 47900 Portola Ave., Palm Desert. Tel. 760/346-5694. Open daily Jun-Sep 7am-1:30pm, Oct-May 8am-5pm. Admission: $34.95, ages 3-12 $24.95, under 3 free. Closed Dec 25. Parking is included in the entrance price. Private Safari tour from $71, ages 3-12 from $44 (must be booked in advance). www.livingdesert.org.

MID-CENTURY MODERN ARCHITECTURE

It's safe to say that Palm Springs has the largest concentration of mid-century modern architecture in the country. As Hollywood celebrities (and their money) began to flock to the area, architects of the new movement—dubbed Desert Modernism—became famous in their own right. These superstar architects—among them Albert Frey, Donald Wexler, E. Stewart Williams, William Cody, John Lautner, and Richard Neutra—blurred the lines between indoors and out, achieving an almost seamless integration between their structures and the environment. They incorporated industrial building materials like concrete, steel, and glass with low-profile design. So grab a cocktail, relax poolside, and enjoy some of the best mid-century modern Palm Springs has to offer. (*See map on next page for locations.*)

Alexander Steel Houses

On the north side of Palm Springs, you'll find seven mid-century modern homes. In 1962, Donald Wexler and Ric Harrison created an all-steel system for prefabricated homes. Built by the Alexander Construction Company and located in a remote, windy part of the city, the homes, primarily composed of steel and glass panels, were marketed as affordable for the middle class. After years of neglect, they have now been restored. *Info*: 3100 block of N. Sunnyview Dr. The homes can be reached by exiting N. Indian Canyon Dr. onto E. Simms Rd.

Santa Fe Savings & Loan (now the Architectural Design Center of the Palm Springs Art Museum) and **Albert Frey House II**. *Info*: See the entry and photos in this book for the Palm Springs Art Museum on page 15.

Tramway Gas Station (now the Palm Springs Visitor Center). *Info*: See the photo and entry on page 12.

PALM SPRINGS/COACHELLA VALLEY

Mid-Century Modern
1. Albert Frey House II
2. Alexander Steel Houses
3. Architecture Design Center/ Santa Fe Savings & Loan
4. City Hall
5. City National Bank
6. Coachella Valley Savings and Loan (Number 2)
7. Del Marcos Hotel
8. Elrod House
9. Kaufmann House
10. Kocher Samson Building
11. Monkey Tree Hotel
12. Racquet Club Cottages West
13. St. Theresa Catholic Church
14. Ship of the Desert
15. The Bob Hope Residence
16. Tramway Gas Station (Visitor Center)

City Hall

The fabulous Palm Springs City Hall—definitely *not* your standard-issue government building—was a collaboration of architectural heavyweights Albert Frey, E. Stewart Williams, Robson Chambers, and John Porter Clark. The screen wall in front, made of metal tubing cut at angles and stacked in rows, serves as a defense against the intense morning sun. This screen design can be found on many buildings in the city. And does *your* city hall have palm trees shooting through the front entryway? (We didn't think so.) *Info*: 3200 E. Tahquitz Way.

City National Bank

When the City National Bank building opened, *Southwest Builder and Contractor* called it "one of the most dramatic structures to rise in Southern California" and "the most beautiful bank in America." Designed in 1958 by Rudi Baumfeld of Victor Gruen and Associates, this mid-century modern gem features a curved exterior and striking blue glass mosaic tile. Today it is home to a branch of the Bank of America. *Info*: 588 S. Palm Canyon Dr. (at the corner of Ramon Rd.). *Currently being renovated.*

PALM SPRINGS/COACHELLA VALLEY 21

Coachella Valley Savings and Loan (Number 2)
This historic building is an example of the International Style of architecture. Designed by architect E. Stewart Williams in 1960, it features a flat roof, steel-frame construction, little ornamentation, and inverted concrete arches. Today it's the home of a branch of Chase Bank. *Info*: 499 S. Palm Canyon Dr.

Nearby is another **Coachella Valley Savings and Loan** building. Designed in 1955 by E. Stewart Williams, this former bank is now an event space. The black terrazzo floors, terrazzo staircase, and circular walk-in bank vault all remain. *Info*: 383 S. Palm Canyon Dr.

Del Marcos Hotel
Designed by William F. Cody in 1947, this 17-room modernist hotel is found in the Tennis Club neighborhood near downtown. Built of stone and redwood, the rooms were designed to surround the pool and show off the stunning mountain views. *Info*: 225 W. Baristo Rd. (at S. Belardo Rd.).

Elrod House
Look familiar? This residence was featured in the James Bond film *Diamonds Are Forever* and in photo shoots for *Playboy Magazine*. It was designed in 1968 by John Lautner on the edge of a hill in the south side of the city, and is named for interior designer Arthur Elrod, the original owner. It's an example of "free architecture," where architecture and nature are combined. Boulders are part of the interior of the house, and run through the walls and windows. It also has a circular living room, sliding glass walls, and an incredible infinity pool. *Info*: 2175 Southridge Dr.

Kaufmann House
Many consider this the most famous mid-century modern home in Palm Springs. Designed by architect Richard Neutra in 1946, the home celebrates a connection to the desert landscape, with large sliding-glass walls that opened interior living spaces to outdoor patios. The home was built for Edgar J. Kaufmann, Sr., a Pittsburgh businessman, as a desert retreat from brutal winters. It was made famous by photos taken by Julius Shulman and Slim Aarons of ladies of leisure sipping cocktails poolside. Shockingly, the house stood vacant for several years after Kaufmann's death in 1955. Fortunately, it's been lovingly renovated by several famous owners, including singer Barry Manilow. Truly a remarkable mid-century modern home. *Info*: 470 W. Vista Chino.

Kocher Samson Building
Albert Frey and A. Lawrence Kocher designed this building in 1934 for Kocher's brother, who needed a location for his medical practice. Designed to have commercial spaces on the ground floor and a small apartment on the second floor, the International Style structure has plate-glass windows, minimal overhangs, stucco finish, steel-framed windows, a flat roof, and a courtyard between the two offices on the ground floor. The building is in the Uptown Design District. *Info*: 766 North Palm Canyon Dr.

Monkey Tree Hotel
Designed by Albert Frey in 1960, The Monkey Tree is an excellent example of mid-century modern architecture. Recently renovated with retro styling and vintage decor, take a trip back in time and imagine its former guests (including Bob Hope, President Kennedy, Marilyn Monroe, and Lucille Ball) hanging out poolside. Groovy! *Info*: 2388 E Racquet Club Rd.

Racquet Club Cottages West
Constructed on land adjacent to the world-famous Racquet Club (now in disrepair), the Racquet Club Cottages West complex (now known as the Racquet Club Garden Villas) is a collection of 37 modernist homes designed by William F. Cody in the 1950s. They feature floor-to-ceiling sliding glass doors, exposed beams, patios, and signature low profiles, and are set among a lush landscape of palm trees, curved pathways, and winding streams. *Info*: 360 West Cabrillo Road (off Racquet Club Dr.).

St. Theresa Catholic Church
Designed by parishioner William F. Cody, the church, with its distinct soaring spire, was dedicated in 1968, and was one of Cody's last projects. Cody's funeral mass took place here, as well as the service for former mayor and Congressman Sonny Bono.
Info: 2800 E. Ramon Rd.

Ship of the Desert
Adrian Wilson and Eric Webster designed this nautical-themed house in 1936. The living room looks like the bow of an ocean liner that ran aground in the middle of the desert. The home is located in the Mesa neighborhood.
Info: 1995 S. Camino Monte (in the gated community of Southridge).

The Bob Hope Home
Designed by Modernist architect John Lautner for entertainer Bob Hope and his wife Delores, construction of this massive 24,000-square-foot (2,300-square-meter) home began in 1979. Many think it looks like a spaceship, although it was actually inspired by the shape of a volcano.
Info: 2466 Southridge Dr. (gated community). To get a close look, you can hike the Araby Trail which takes you past the property. It's a moderate, three-mile (4.8 km) loop.

MODERNISM WEEK

Modernism Week is a celebration of mid-century modern design, architecture, fashion, art, and culture. The festival, held in February, includes architectural walking and home tours, lectures, and (of course) cocktail parties. There is also the annual Palm Springs Modernism Show & Sale with world-class exhibitors. This event has grown each year, and has now added a fall preview in October. For a list of all the events, visit www.modernismweek.com.

MOORTEN BOTANICAL GARDEN AND CACTARIUM

A favorite of ours, this family-owned botanical garden, located in a mostly residential neighborhood, showcases amazing desert plants from around the world. Chester Moorten, one of the original silent-movie "Keystone Kops," and his wife Patricia, a botanist and flower-shop owner, opened a one-acre nursery on this spot in 1939, and it's still going strong. Enjoy a meandering stroll through the garden, or request a guided tour. Stop by the "Cactarium" greenhouse, filled with all manner of desert cacti and succulents. Then there's the Moortens' gorgeous, Mediterranean-style home, the fabulous "Cactus Castle," overlooking a quiet corner of the grounds. And if you simply can't get enough, you can purchase your very own cactus, grown right on the premises, to take home with you. (Unfortunately, the live tortoises aren't for sale—but they just might be enjoying a nice broccoli salad when you visit.) We love this quirky place! *Info*: 1701 S. Palm Canyon Dr., Palm Springs. Tel. 760/327-6555. Open Thu-Tue 10am-4pm. Closed Wed. Jun-Sep Fri-Sun 9am-1pm. Admission: $5, ages 5-15 $2. www.moortenbotanicalgarden.com.

SUNNYLANDS
This classic 200-acre, mid-century modern estate was the winter residence of Walter and Leonore Annenberg. Walter owned a publishing empire that included *TV Guide*, *Playboy*, *The Saturday Evening Post*, and *Seventeen* magazines. He served as Ambassador to the United Kingdom under President Richard Nixon, who retreated to Sunnylands the day he was pardoned—only one of the hundreds of notable guests who visited over the years. A. Quincy Jones, a well-known mid-century modern architect, designed the home; the entire project, including the grounds, was completed in 1966. The estate included a pool (of course), 13 man-made lakes, a tennis court, a nine-hole golf course, and a nine-acre desert garden. Landscape architect James Burnett, who designed the grounds, said he'd been inspired by the Annenbergs' extensive art collection, including works by van Gogh and Cezanne.

Garden visits are free, don't require a reservation, and include a 20-minute film, *A Place Called Sunnylands*. But if you'd like to see the home, you'll need to reserve a spot on the *Historic House Tour* shuttle—a 90-minute guided tour through the residence, including the art collection. Or grab your binoculars and take the *Birding on the Estate* shuttle tour, with an expert birder as your guide. Or maybe you'd like the *Open-Air Experience*, a 45-minute guided shuttle tour of the grounds, including the estate's outdoor sculptures. For information and reservations, visit www.sunnylands.org. And take note: You'll need to plan months in advance! *Info:* 37977 Bob Hope Dr., Rancho Mirage. Tel. 760/202-2222. Gardens open Wed-Sun 8:30am-4pm, closed in summer. Admission from $26. Gardens are free. *Historic House Tour* $55, *Open-Air Experience* $28, and *Birding on the Estate* $39.

PALM SPRINGS/COACHELLA VALLEY 27

WINDMILL TOURS
If you're driving to the Coachella Valley by car, you can't miss the wind turbines along Interstate 10—there are almost 2,000 of them! And if you'd like to get up close to them—and learn more about renewable energy—the Palm Springs Self-Driving Windmill Tour is just the ticket. The approximately one-hour, self-guided tour begins at headquarters, with a short history of the windmills. Then you'll be given a tablet to guide you through ten marked stops, including a display yard of non-operating turbines (many of them failed designs), a generating wind turbine, and a solar farm. But hold on to your hat: It's windy out there! *Info*: 62950 20th Ave., Palm Springs. Tel. 800/531-5834. Open daily 9am-2pm. You must reserve in advance. Tours start at $59 per vehicle (includes two people, each additional person is $10). Guided tours on a golf cart $55 per person. From Palm Springs head north on N. Indian Canyon Dr., cross the I-10 freeway, then turn left onto 20th Avenue. Drive approximately one mile (1.6 km), you'll see the Windmill Tours headquarters on the right. www.windmilltours.com.

FOREVER MARILYN
Forever Marilyn is a 26-foot-tall (eight meters) statue made of stainless steel and aluminum. Created by Seward Johnson, it captures the famous image of Marilyn Monroe in a billowing white dress as she stands over a subway grate in the 1955 film *The Seven Year Itch*. Line up with others to get a photo at this popular downtown destination honoring an icon who was discovered in Palm Springs. *Info*: Museum Way (in front of the Palm Springs Art Museum).

AGUA CALIENTE CULTURAL MUSEUM/AGUA CALIENTE CULTURAL PLAZA

Over 2,000 years ago, the Agua Caliente Band of Cahuilla Indians settled in the Indian Canyons (south of what is now downtown Palm Springs). Opening in 2023, the Agua Caliente Cultural Museum will be part of the Agua Caliente Cultural Plaza, whose design was inspired by the desert landscape and traditional Agua Caliente crafts. Enjoy the museum, visit the gardens and spa (a nod to the healing waters of the Agua Caliente Hot Mineral Spring), explore the Oasis Trail—or simply share in the spirit of community. You can be pampered and soak in the ancient hot mineral spring at **The Spa at Séc-he**. *Info*: Corner of S. Indian Canyon Dr. and Tahquitz Canyon Way. Tel. 760/778-1079. Open Tue-Sun 10am-5pm. Closed Mon. www.accmuseum.org. Spa open daily 8am-7pm. Reservations 866/777-3243. thespaatseche.com.

VILLAGE GREEN HERITAGE CENTER

Located among downtown restaurants and shops, the Palm Springs Historical Society, based in the two oldest homes in the city, offers a fascinating look into the past. You'll find:

• **The Cornelia White House**
Pioneer Cornelia White lived here. Built in 1893, the house was originally part of the Palm Springs Hotel, the first hotel in the area.

• **The McCallum Adobe**
Dating back to 1884, this was the home of the first pioneer family to the area. It's now a museum dedicated to the history of Palm Springs and includes hundreds of photographs documenting the city from the 1880s to present.

• **Ruddy's 1930s General Store**
This is a replica of a general store from before Palm Springs was incorporated as a city. You'll find a collection of 1930s groceries, household goods, and medicines stocked on its shelves.

The historical society also offers walking tours through the city's interesting neighborhoods. Tours can be booked by reserving at 760/844-2242 or www.pshistoricalsociety.org, and begin at $35.

The society also operates a historical library and visitors center in the Welwood Murray Memorial Library at 100 S. Palm Canyon Dr. Tel. 760-656-7394. Open daily 10am-6pm.

ELVIS HONEYMOON HIDEAWAY
Originally designed by William Krisel for developer Robert Alexander and his family, the "House of Tomorrow"—three stories of four concentric circles under a boomerang-shaped roof—was so "groovy," Elvis and Priscilla Presley honeymooned here in 1967. Elvis reportedly carried Priscilla through the front door singing the "Hawaiian Wedding Song." The home is on a quiet cul-de-sac in the Vista Las Palmas neighborhood. *Info*: 1350 Ladera Circle, Palm Springs. Tours are offered during Modernism Week.

ARENAS ROAD AND THE LGBTQ+ SCENE

Palm Springs is a big destination for LGBTQ+ visitors. The city has one of the highest concentrations of gay residents in the U.S. and, in 2017, Palm Springs elected the country's first all-LGBTQ+ city council. Gay life here is vibrant and varied.

Most of the venues are on or around Arenas Road in downtown Palm Springs. Here are some of the fun destinations:

- **Hunters**, 302 E. Arenas Rd. www.hunterspalmsprings.com. This gay club draws a mostly male crowd and features a popular dance floor. On weekends, you'll also find quite a few bridal parties.
- **Quadz**, 200 S. Indian Canyon Dr. (enter off Arenas Rd.). www.quadz.bar. This popular bar features show tunes, theme nights, and karaoke.
- **Chill**, 217 E. Arenas Rd. www.chillbarpalmsprings.com. Contemporary bar with an outdoor patio. You can dance on weekend nights at its Scorpion Room.
- **Dick's**, 301 E. Arenas Rd. www.dicksps.com. This Levi/leather bar is a new edition to the bar scene. Daily drink specials.
- **Streetbar**, 224 E. Arenas Rd. www.facebook.com/psstreetbar. Catering to an older male crowd, this bar also has karaoke and live performances.
- **Blackbook**, 315 E. Arenas Rd. www.blackbookbar.com. Drinks and bar food at this sleekly designed space.
- **Oscar's**, 125 E. Tahquitz Canyon Way (a block off Arenas Rd.). www.oscarspalmsprings.com. Casual dining on the patio, daily happy hour, and a wildly popular tea dance on Sundays.

There are also several shops on the street, including **Gay Mart** (305 E. Arenas Rd.) for all your gay needs, with a large clothing collection. gaymart.business.site. **Bear Wear** (319 E. Arenas Rd) offers clothing, swimwear, gifts, and caps. bear-wear-etc.shoplightspeed.com.

Although many of the gay establishments are centered around Arenas Rd., others are scattered around town and in Cathedral City.

- **Toucan's Tiki Lounge**, 2100 N Palm Canyon Dr., Palm Springs, www.toucanstikilounge.com. This fun bar with tropical decor features fabulous drag shows and a dance floor.
- **Tool Shed**, 600 E. Sunny Dunes Rd., Palm Springs, www.pstoolshed.com. Levi/leather bar with a lot of cruising. Popular underwear night on Thursday.
- **The Roost Lounge**, 68718 E Palm Canyon Dr., Cathedral City. www.theroostcc.com. Bar, video lounge, and stage for performances (including drag shows).
- **One Eleven Bar**, 67555 E Palm Canyon Dr., Cathedral City, oneelevenbar.com. Laid-back cocktail lounge with frequent live performances.
- **The Barracks**, 67-625 E. Palm Canyon Dr., Cathedral City, www.barracksps.com. Leather bar with popular underwear night on Wednesdays and Sunday beer bust.
- **Runway**, 68300 Gay Resort Dr., Cathedral City, www.runwayccbc.com. Bar and restaurant connected to the CCBC resort.

For information on the many LGBTQ+ resorts in and around Palm Springs, see page 100 of the Sleeping section of this book.

LGBTQ+ EVENTS

Palm Springs has three events that draw thousands of LGBTQ+ visitors to the city. **Pride**, held the first weekend in November, has a fun festival and a Sunday parade that attracts over 60,000 people. www.pspride.info. **White Party** for gay men (www.whitepartyglobal.com) and **The Dinah** for lesbians (www.thedinah.com) take place every year. There are many other specialty events, such as Bear and Blatino weekends. A good source for events is the Gay Desert Guide (www.gaydesertguide.com).

MUSEUM OF ANCIENT WONDERS (MoAW)
This new museum, in a strip mall in Cathedral City, houses 375 artifacts. The King Tut exhibit features reproductions of his treasures, including throne and chariot. There are also authentic artifacts from this period of Egyptian history. The museum has four full-size dinosaur casts, African tribal masks, and fossils. A captivating museum in an unexpected location. *Info*: 69028-B E. Palm Canyon Dr. in Cathedral City. Tel. 442/268-5004. Open Sat-Wed 10am-6pm, Sun noon-5pm. Admission: $15. www.moaw.org.

CASINOS
Get ready to lose some money! Or perhaps you'd rather dine, drink, or see a show. The Coachella Valley is dotted with tribal casinos. Try your luck at one of these:

Spa Resort Casino
Located in downtown Palm Springs, this casino has slot machines and table games. You'll also find a lounge, casual dining, and a steakhouse. There's no longer a hotel here, but this casino has plenty of parking and is near many hotels. *Info*: 401 E. Amado Rd. Tel. 888/999-1995. www.aguacalientecasinos.com.

Morongo Casino Resort and Spa
You can't miss this huge casino and hotel if you are arriving from Los Angeles on Interstate 10. Located 18 miles (29 km) west of Palm Springs in Cabazon (known for its large discount shopping center), this huge casino feels like you're in Las Vegas. There's a bowling center, plenty of dining options, and a golf club. *Info*: 49500 Seminole Dr., Cabazon. Tel. 951/849-3080. www.morongocasinoresort.com.

Spotlight 29 Casino
This casino, in Coachella, is known for its entertainment venue. Slot machines, table games, and plenty of dining options. *Info*: 46-200 Harrison Pl., Coachella. Tel. 760/775-5566. www.spotlight29.com.

Tortoise Rock Casino
This casino is located north of Joshua Tree National Park in Twentynine Palms. It's open 24 hours and has slot machines, table games, and casual dining. *Info*: 73829 Baseline Rd., Twentynine Palms. Tel. 760/367-9759. www.tortoiserockcasino.com.

PALM SPRINGS/COACHELLA VALLEY

Agua Caliente Casino Resort
Also off I-10, this modern casino and hotel is located 10 miles (16 km) outside of Palm Springs in Rancho Mirage. Slot machines, table games, poker room, and a high-limit room. Lots of dining options. There's a theater for live concerts and performances. *Info*: 32-250 Bob Hope Dr., Rancho Mirage. Tel. 760/321-2000. www.aguacalientecasinos.com.

Agua Caliente Cathedral City
A recent addition to the casino scene, this Agua Caliente venue is in downtown Cathedral City, and features slot machines and table games. Plenty of parking available at its location off California route 111. Like its sister casino in Rancho Mirage, it also has a sports bar (360 Sports). There's a large outdoor pavilion which hosts live entertainment and food trucks. Upscale dining at Café One Eleven, and coffee, salads, and lighter fare at casual Java Caliente. *Info*: 68960 E. Palm Canyon Dr., Cathedral City. Tel. 888/999-1995. Open 24 hours daily. www.aguacalientecasinos.com.

Fantasy Springs Resort Casino
This large complex in Indio has slot machines and table games. There's also a hotel, plenty of dining options, golfing, bowling, and a theater. *Info:* 84-245 Indio Springs Parkway, Indio. Tel. 800/827-2946. www.fantasyspringsresort.com.

34 PALM SPRINGS MADE EASY

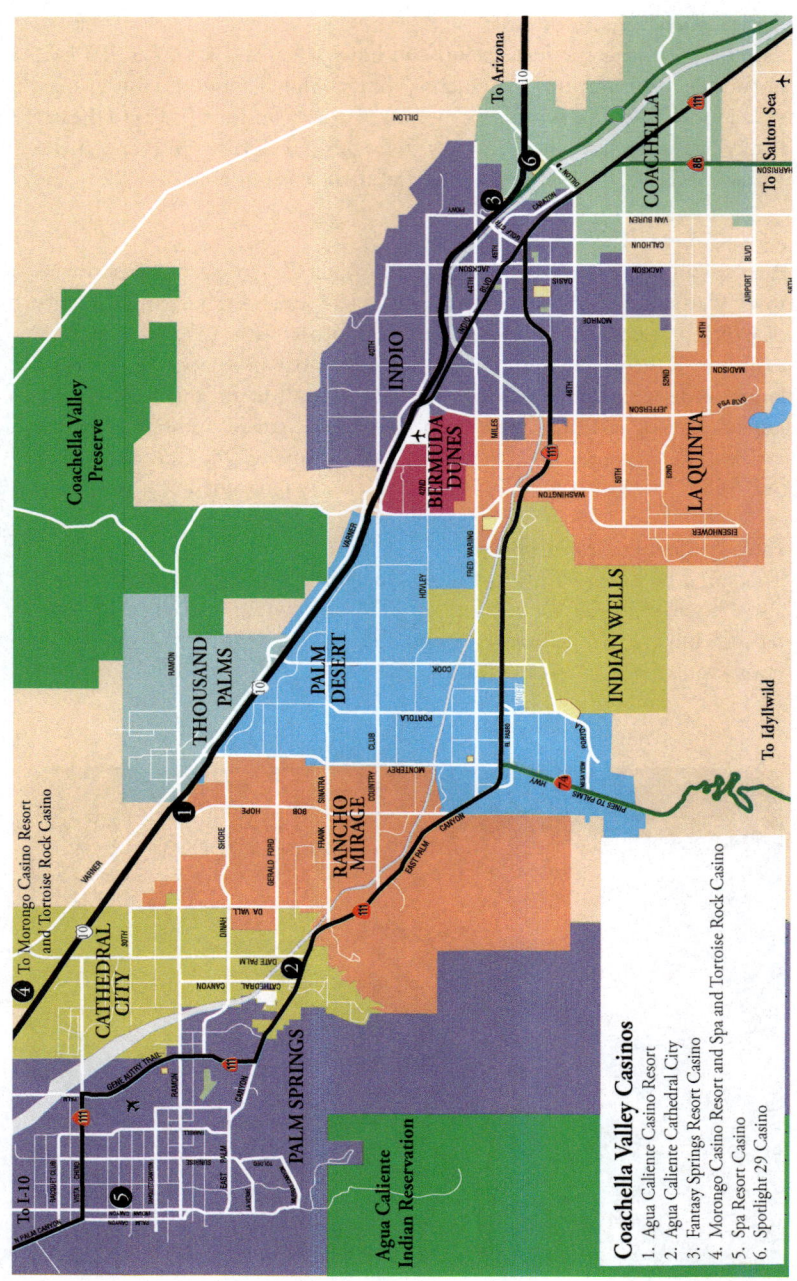

Coachella Valley Casinos
1. Agua Caliente Casino Resort
2. Agua Caliente Cathedral City
3. Fantasy Springs Resort Casino
4. Morongo Casino Resort and Spa and Tortoise Rock Casino
5. Spa Resort Casino
6. Spotlight 29 Casino

PALM SPRINGS/COACHELLA VALLEY 35

POOL SCENE
Whether you're visiting friends, renting a home, or staying in a hotel, you'll likely have access to a pool where you can start your day with a refreshing dip, spend your day lounging, or relax after a day of sightseeing. Some hotels in the city allow non-guests to hang out at the pool (with the added benefit of poolside bars!). Here are a few to check out. Day passes can also be booked through resortpass.com.

Ace Hotel & Swim Club
The large pool here holds frequent weekend deejay parties, complete with poolside food and drink service. There's also the "Feel Good Spa," if you're feeling stressed out. And when it gets too hot, cool off inside with a classic cocktail at the Amigo Room. Non-hotel guests can often purchase daily pool passes from $45. *Info*: 701 E. Palm Canyon Dr., Tel. 760/325-9900. www.acehotel.com/palm-springs.

ARRIVE
This hotel on the northern end of town allows guests and locals alike to hang out at the pool. You can rent a cabana, or just relax poolside with drinks. In the summer, there's "Dive In Movie" night, where you can watch an old-time favorite while floating in the pool. Note: During special events, weekends, and high season, the hotel sometimes limits the number of non-guests. The **Palm Canyon Swim & Social** is an adults-only poolside restaurant and bar serving an all-day brunch *Info*: 1551 N. Palm Canyon Dr. Tel. 760/507-1640. Reserved lounger day pass from $40. www.arrivehotels.com.

Saguaro
The hotel pool at this colorful hotel has two hot tubs and an outdoor bar–and can get quite crowded. The weekend pool parties showcase some of the best-known deejays spinning dance music. From $40. *Info*: 1800 E. Palm Canyon Dr. Tel. 760/323-1711. www.thesaguaro.com.

Rowan
Boasting the only one in the city, the rooftop pool at Rowan Kimpton Hotel offers spectacular views of the mountains and downtown Palm Springs. Cabana rentals from $150, plus a $200 food and drink minimum (for six people). The **High Bar** serves pricey snacks and cocktails. This is your upscale pool choice. *Info*: 100 W. Tahquitz Canyon Way. Tel. 760/904-5015. www.rowanpalmsprings.com.

El Morocco Inn & Spa
For a novel experience, relax in the hot natural mineral springs at this Moroccan-themed inn located in nearby Desert Hot Springs. Day-spa guests have access to the pool, spa, and two dry saunas. A locker, robe, and towel are included, along with coffee, tea, water, and healthy snacks. *Info*: 66810 4th St. Tel. 760/288-2527. www.elmoroccoinn.com. Admission: $60.

SPLASH HOUSE

The ultimate pool party takes place several weekends each summer and is hosted by three hotels in Palm Springs. In past years it has been held at Saguaro, Renaissance, and Margaritaville.

You buy a pass or hotel package that gives you admission to all resorts for the weekend. There's an additional charge to dance the night away after hours at the Palm Springs Air Museum. Shuttles run between all hotel venues and to the after hours parties at the Palm Springs Air Museum. *Info*: General admission wristband from $210. Tickets for the after hours party from $60. www.splashhouse.com.

PALM SPRINGS/COACHELLA VALLEY 37

Pools
1. Ace Hotel & Swim Club
2. ARRIVE
3. Saguaro
4. Rowan
5. El Morocco Inn & Spa
6. Riviera/Margaritaville

THE HOLLYWOOD CONNECTION

Under the Hollywood studio system, stars were required to report to work on short notice. A rule, allegedly written into many contracts, was that an actor or actress could not travel more than two hours or 100 miles (161 km) from the set when they were not needed during filming. Conveniently, Palm Springs was within 100 miles from Hollywood—and the city became the "Playground of the Stars."

The Homes of the Stars

The **Vista Las Palmas** and **Old Las Palmas** neighborhoods have the highest concentration of celebrity homes in Palm Springs. Leonardo DiCaprio, Kirk Douglas, Katharine Hepburn, Elizabeth Taylor, Cary Grant, and Dinah Shore are just a few of the stars who have or had homes in these neighborhoods.

So, if you're looking to see the largest number of celebrity homes in the shortest amount of time, here is where you'll head! We've also included celebrity homes in other neighborhoods.

These celebrity homes are listed by neighborhood and in alphabetic order.

Vista Las Palmas/Old Las Palmas/Little Tuscany

Jack Benny: 424 W. Vista Chino
Vaudeville star who became a popular radio, television, and film star.
Cher: 252 Camino Sur
Everyone knows who Cher is!
Cyd Charisse and Tony Martin: 1197 Monte Vista
Actress and dancer (*Singin' in the Rain*) and her actor/singer husband (*Stranger in Paradise*).
Nat King Cole: 1258 Rose Ave
One of the greatest pop vocalists of all time, and a major figure in the development of jazz piano.
Bobby Darin: 845 N. Fair Circle
One of pop music's most well-known vocalists (*Mack The Knife*).

PALM SPRINGS/COACHELLA VALLEY

Sammy Davis, Jr.: 444 Chino Dr.
Talented all-around entertainer, one of the first black artists to find mass appeal (*The Candy Man*), and member of the Rat Pack.
Leonardo DiCaprio: 432 Hermosa
Oscar-winning actor (*The Revenant*).
Kirk Douglas: 515 Via Lola
Famous actor (*Spartacus* and *20,000 Leagues Under the Sea*).
Clark Gable: 222 Chino Dr.
Academy Award-winning actor (*It Happened One Night*).
Zsa Zsa Gabor: 595 W. Chino Canyon Dr.
Actress and former Miss Hungary. Known for her large personality and many marriages.
Cary Grant: 928 N. Avenida Palmas
Debonair actor during Hollywood's Golden Age.
Katharine Hepburn and Spencer Tracy: 766 Mission Rd.
They won multiple Academy Awards (*On Golden Pond* and *Boys Town*).
Howard Hughes: 335 Camino Norte
Reclusive businessman and film director.
Bob Hope: 1188 E. El Alameda
One of three properties owned by the entertainer.
Alan Ladd: 323 Camino Norte
Producer and actor (*Shane*).
Peter Lawford/Patricia Kennedy: 1295 N. Via Monte Vista
Member of the Rat Pack/JFK's sister.
Liberace: 226 Alejo Rd./501 Belardo Rd.
Liberace Guest House: 1441 N. Kaweah Rd.
Flamboyant pianist (*see photo at right*).
Dean Martin: 1123 Monte Vista
Singer, actor, and member of the Rat Pack.
Mary Martin: 365 Camino Norte
Tony Award and Emmy Award-winning actress (*South Pacific*).
Ann Miller: 457 Hermosa Pl.
Dancer, singer, and actress best known for her work in Hollywood musicals of the 1940s and 1950s.
Elvis and Priscilla Honeymoon Hideaway: 1350 Ladera Circle (*see page 29*)
Elvis Presley: 845 Chino Canyon
Film and music icon, aka the "King."
Ronald and Nancy Reagan: 369 Hermosa Pl.
40th president of the United States and his actress wife.
Debbie Reynolds: 670 Stevens Rd.
Singer and actress (*Singin' in the Rain*).

40 PALM SPRINGS MADE EASY

Edward G. Robinson: 999 N. Patencio
Stage and screen actor during Hollywood's Golden Age.
Sydney Sheldon: 425 Via Lola
Director, producer, and writer of best-selling romantic suspense novels (*Master of the Game*).
Dinah Shore and George Montgomery: 317 Camino Norte
She was a singer, actress, and television personality (*Dinah!*) and he an actor in Western films and television.
Frank Sinatra: 1148 E. Alejo Rd.
One of several homes owned by the singer and actor.
Barbra Streisand and James Brolin: 555 Patencio Rd.
Oscar-, Tony-, and Grammy-Award winner Streisand and actor Brolin.
Elizabeth Taylor: 417 W. Hermosa Pl.
Screen legend and Academy-Award winner (*Butterfield 8* and *Who's Afraid of Virginia Woolf?*). (*pictured at right*)

Movie Colony
Lucille Ball: 1194 N. Via Miraleste
Comedic legend, incredible businesswoman, and one of television's earliest superstars.
Truman Capote: 853 E. Paseo El Mirador
Novelist, screenwriter, playwright, and actor. Best known for *Breakfast at Tiffany's* (1958) and *In Cold Blood* (1966).
Bing Crosby: 1011 E. El Alameda
One of the most influential male vocalists of all time.
Tony Curtis: 641 N. Camino Real
Actor whose career spanned six decades (*Some Like It Hot*).
Frank Sinatra: 1148 East Alejo Rd. (*pictured on the next page*)
Famous singer, actor, and member of the Rat Pack.

Other Neighborhoods
Sonny Bono: 294 Crestview Dr.
Actor, singer, former mayor, and Congressman. Best known as half of Sonny & Cher.

Walt Disney: 2688 S. Camino Real
Businessman, animator, writer, and film producer who holds the record for most Academy Awards earned by an individual.
Eddie Fisher and Debbie Reynolds: 955 La Jolla Rd
He was one of the most popular singers of the 1950s, and she was a much-loved singer and actress (*The Unsinkable Molly Brown*).
Eva Gabor: 1509 S. Manzanita Ave.
Actress in film and television (*Green Acres*).
Steve McQueen: 811 E. Grace Circle
Once the highest-paid movie star (*The Great Escape*).
Sia: 232 Avenida Ortega
Singer and songwriter (*Chandelier*). The property, called Fontanelle, was originally owned by Max Factor.
Suzanne Somers: 252 Ridge Rd.
Television actress (*Three's Company*) and self-help author.
Loretta Young: 1075 Manzanita Ave.
Academy-Award winner (*The Farmer's Daughter*) and television star (*The Loretta Young Show*).

DESERT MEMORIAL PARK
Flat and uniform grave stones, under shade trees, mark the remains of some of Hollywood's most famous celebrities. Frank Sinatra, Sonny Bono, and the Gabors are among the stars buried here. *Info*: 31750 Da Vall Dr., Cathedral City. Tel. 760/328-3316. Open daily 7am-4:40pm. Map available at the office. pscemetery.com.

Walk of the Stars
Since 1992, over 440 people—entertainers, architects, authors, humanitarians, civic leaders, artists, and athletes— have been honored on the sidewalks throughout Palm Springs, primarily located on Palm Canyon Drive, Tahquitz Canyon

Way, and Museum Drive. Some of the notable honorees include Shirley Temple, Mary Pickford, Clark Gable, Bob Hope, Frank Sinatra, Ginger Rogers, Gene Autry, Liberace, Elizabeth Taylor, Elvis Presley, Dinah Shore, Sonny Bono, Merv Griffin, Ronald Reagan, Gerald Ford, Lily Tomlin, Debbie Gibson, Lynda Carter, Carol Channing, and Pierre Cardin. For a full list of stars, check out the walk website. *Info*: You can download the excellent and detailed Palm Springs Walk of the Stars app. LGBTQ+ stars are highlighted with a pride flag emblem. 760/325-1577. www.walkofthestars.com.

Film Festivals
Palm Springs International Film Festival
This film festival was the brainchild of former mayor of Palm Springs Sonny Bono. It has incredible importance in the film industry, as it occurs every January during Academy-Awards voting. Over 12 days, nearly 150,000 people attend the festival, to view over 200 films from nearly 80 countries. The highlight is the Film Awards Gala, where the spotlight is on those who are hoping for an Oscar. *Info*: www.psfilmfest.org.

Other film festivals in the city include:

Palm Springs International ShortFest: Every June, showcasing the best in short films. www.psfilmfest.org.

American Documentary Film Fest: Every March/April, featuring the best of global documentary films. www.amdocfilmfest.com.

Cinema Diverse: Every September, featuring LGBTQ films and hosting fantastic themed parties. www.palmspringsculturalcenter.org/filmfest and cinemadiversethepalmspringslgbtqfilmfestival.festivee.com.

RAT PACK

The Rat Pack was a group of famous entertainers that included Frank Sinatra, Dean Martin, Peter Lawford, Sammy Davis Jr., and Joey Bishop. Shirley MacLaine, Marilyn Monroe, and Angie Dickinson were often referred to as the "Rat Pack Mascots." Some of them even appeared together in films such as *Ocean's 11*, *Robin and the 7 Hoods*, and *Some Came Running*. In the late 1950s and 1960s, the Rat Pack spent much of their time in Palm Springs.

The **Purple Room** is where the Rat Pack cavorted, on and off the stage. You can still enjoy live entertainment while you dine and enjoy classic cocktails. *Info*: 1900 E. Palm Canyon Dr.. Tel. 760/322-4422. Open daily. Closed part of the summer. www.purpleroompalmsprings.com.

Other hangouts of the Rat Pack include what is now the Caliente Tropics Resort (www.calientetropics.com), the Riviera/Margaritaville (www.margaritaville.com), and Melvyn's Restaurant at the Ingleside Inn, with its lively piano bar (www.inglesideinn.com/Melvyns).

HIKING

While most people think of pools, cocktails, and parties, Palm Springs is also a big destination for hikers. You'll not only get your exercise, you'll have panoramic views of the city and the Coachella Valley—and you'll find hiking trails for every fitness level.

Hiking is best from October through April, when temperatures are not hellishly hot. If you choose to hike outside this time, make sure you leave early. Hiking in the summer in Palm Springs is not only hot, it's dangerous. Make sure you wear good shoes and take plenty of water! Here are some of our favorite trails:

Desert Palisades/Chino Cone
This little-known hiking trail is located in north Palm Springs at the west end of Racquet Club Road. The high-end subdivision Desert Palisades commands impressive views of Palm Springs.

As part of the agreement to allow the residential development, the city required that the trails be maintained and open to the public. This is perhaps the highest subdivision in Palm Springs. There are only a handful of homes being built on the 100 lots here, so you feel like you're walking in solitude.

There are markers for the Chino Canyon Trail, established by the Cahuilla Indians, for their migration from the hot springs (in what is now downtown Palm Springs) to cooler upper elevations. Chino Cone is here, a geological formation called an alluvial fan, formed over thousands of years by earthquakes and running water from the San Jacinto Mountains.

PALM SPRINGS/COACHELLA VALLEY 45

Hiking
1. Araby Trail
2. Chino Cove/ Desert Palisades
3. Indian Canyons
4. Museum Trail
5. North Lykken Trail
6. South Lykken Trail
7. Tahquitz Canyon

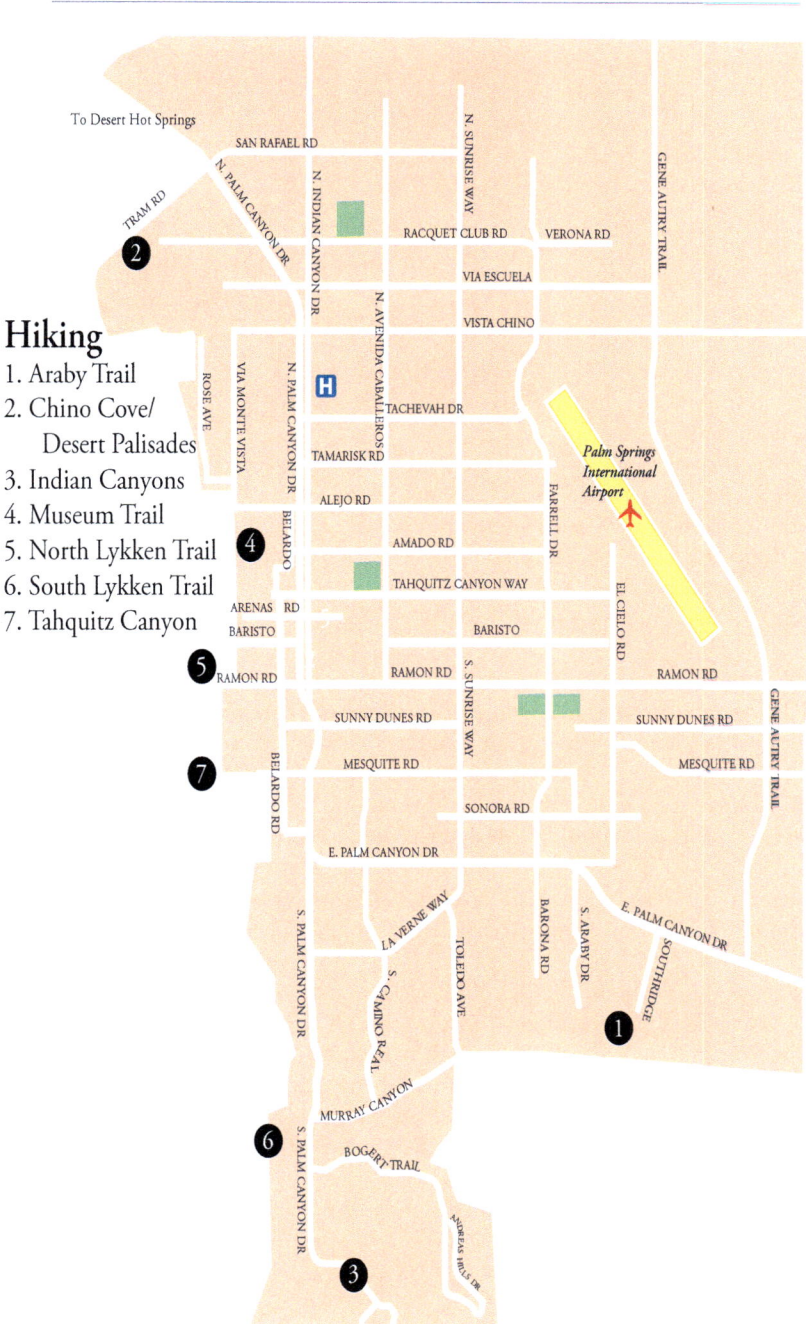

A wonderful, little-used area for moderate hikers. Highly recommended! *Info*: At the western end of Racquet Club Road. Approximately one mile (1.6 km). You can also walk through the neighborhood for several miles on paved streets.

Museum Trail
From the Art Museum, you'll navigate switchbacks up the rocky hillside until you reach the summit. It's fun, popular, and short. You'll be rewarded with great views from the picnic table at the summit. This can be a difficult hike for some, but a wonderful Palm Springs experience. *Info*: Begin at the parking lot of the Palm Springs Art Museum. Two miles (3.2 km) round-trip. Elevation increase: 1,000 feet (305 meters).

North Carl Lykken Trail
This five-mile (8 km) hike affords great views of Palm Springs. The trail is accessible from the west end of Ramon Rd., where there is limited parking. From the Ramon Rd. entrance, the trail takes you up and meanders for about a mile and a half (2.4 km), where you will find picnic tables that are also accessible from the Museum Trail (*see above*).

You can continue on this trail into Chino Canyon, where it wanders along the side of the mountain and deposits you on W. Cielo Rd.

To begin the walk on W. Cielo Rd. in the northern part of Palm Springs, follow these directions. From downtown, head north on N. Palm Canyon Dr. Turn left at Vista Chino Rd. Turn right on Via Norte, then left on Chino Canyon Rd. Veer left onto Panorama Rd., then left again on W. Cielo Rd. This is one of the city's most attractive and interesting neighborhoods. If you do start your hike here, the trail is initially quite steep, but gradually levels off.

PALM SPRINGS/COACHELLA VALLEY 47

South Carl Lykken Trail
From the trailhead, switchbacks take you up approximately 600 feet (183 meters) to a lookout point. The trail levels off before you head up another 400 feet (122 meters) above Tahquitz Canyon. From here you can return the way you came. You can also exit an alternative way (it's a steep decline), where you will reach W. Mesquite Ave. *Info*: From downtown, take S. Palm Canyon Dr. The trail begins on the right side of the street south of Canyon Heights Dr. Five miles (8 km) round-trip. Elevation gain 1,000 feet (305 meters).

Araby Trail
This spectacular hike passes some of the most famous and fabulous homes in Palm Springs. You'll pass the Elrod House (where the James Bond film *Diamonds Are Forever* was filmed) and the other-worldly Bob Hope home. Incredible view of Palm Springs! *Info*: Southridge Road/Rim Road in south Palm Springs. Parking is off Highway 111. Three miles (4.8 km) round-trip. Elevation increase: less than 1,000 feet (305 meters).

Indian Canyons
The Indian Canyons, located in the southwest section of Palm Springs, are the ancestral home of the Agua Caliente Band of Cahuilla Indians. Indian Canyons and Tahquitz Canyon (*see below*) are listed on the National Register of Historic Places. Once you reach the Trading Post, you'll have access to three of the four canyons.

Palm Canyon: The largest California fan palm oasis. This easy hike has little increase in elevation (only about 100 feet [30 meters]). It's 2.2 miles (3.5 km) round-trip. Lush, lovely, and interesting.

Andreas Canyon: A two-mile (3.2 km), round-trip trail takes you through hundreds of California fan palms. There's little elevation increase (less than 100 feet [30.5 meters]), and the pools and waterfall make this an enjoyable hike.

Murray Canyon: Cacti, desert willows, and plenty of California fan palms on this four-mile (6.4 km) round-trip hike. You'll have to cross a stream and ultimately will get to the Seven Sisters Waterfall.

Info: 38520 S. Palm Canyon Dr. Tel. 760/323-6018. Open Oct-Jul 4 daily 8am-5pm. Open Jul 5-Sep Fri-Sun 8am-5pm. Admission: $12, over 62 and students with ID $7, ages 6-12 $6, under 6 and military with ID free. www.indian-canyons.com.

Tahquitz Canyon
This canyon is also operated by the Agua Caliente Band of Cahuilla Indians. You'll enter the hiking area from the Tahquitz Visitors Center, and it can be crowded in high season. There's a slight elevation, 250 feet (76 meters), and the route is two miles (3.2 km) round-trip. The trail follows a creek and takes you to a waterfall (dry during summer), and through an ancient Cahuilla village. This fantastic hike is an excellent choice!

Info: You reach the entrance from S. Palm Canyon Dr. and turn right on Mesquite Ave. The center is located at 500 W. Mesquite Ave. Tel. 760/416-7044. Open Oct-Jul 4 daily 7:30am-5pm. Open Jul 5-Sep 30 Fri-Sun 7:30am-5pm. Admission: $15, ages 6-12 $7. Free under 6 and active military with ID. www.tahquitzcanyon.com.

PALM SPRINGS/COACHELLA VALLEY 49

Mount San Jacinto State Park
Take the Aerial Tramway (*see the entry earlier in this chapter*) to the Mountain Station. Here, you'll have access to 54 miles (87 km) of trails spread over 14,000 acres of mountain wilderness. You're required to check in at the Long Valley Ranger Station (just a quarter-mile away from the Mountain Station).

Fill out a day-use permit form (free) here, where it's going to be about 40°F (5°C) cooler than in Palm Springs. You do not have to check in if you're only taking the Long Valley Discovery Trail or the Desert View Trail. Here are a few of the fantastic trails to enjoy:

Long Valley Discovery Trail: This easy half-mile (.8 km) trail is at the bottom of Mountain Station. It may be easy, but some will find the walk back up to the Mountain Station a bit strenuous. Smell the pine trees and check out the signs describing the state park's plants and animals.

Desert View Trail: This mile-and-a-half (2.4 km) hike allows you to expand on the Long Valley Discovery Trail. Stroll through the pine forest, and take in stunning views of the Coachella Valley.

Round Valley: When you register at the Long Valley Ranger Station, you'll follow the Low Trail until you reach the markers for this trail. Walk along a seasonal creek surrounded by pines, and you'll reach Round Valley. If you continue on from the Round Valley Trail, it will take you all the way up to Mount San Jacinto (*see below*). This hike is approximately five miles (8 km) round-trip.

San Jacinto Peak: This strenuous hike is 12 miles (19 km) long round-trip. You'll ultimately reach the peak where you'll have views of not only Palm Springs, but as far away as the Salton Sea. An incredible hike.

BIKING

Palm Springs is a great place to ride a bike, and the city has several well-marked loops. The Downtown Loop begins at N. Palm Canyon and Alejo. It's 3 miles (4.8 km) and runs around downtown and passes the Palm Springs Art Museum. The Deepwell Loop begins at Mesquite and Sunrise. It's 3.5 miles (5.6 km) and takes you through one of the city's oldest neighborhoods. The Citywide Loop begins at N. Palm Canyon and Tachevah. It's 13 miles (21 km) and takes you through residential neighborhoods (including Old Las Palmas), past the Art Museum, and on to the south end of town. There are several other loops, including the Las Palmas Loop, which meanders past the homes of the stars, and the Canyon Country Club Loop, which explores the southern part of the city. Many hotels offer bikes to guests. If yours doesn't, you can rent a bike from the convenient downtown location of BIKE Palm Springs at 194 S. Indian Canyon (at Arenas Rd.). Tel. 760/832-8912. From $35 per day. Electric bikes are also available. www.bikepsrentals.com.

PALM SPRINGS/COACHELLA VALLEY

GOLFING/TENNIS

Palm Springs is a huge destination for golfers. There are well over 100 courses throughout the Coachella Valley. Most of the courses have the added bonus of stunning views of the mountains. If you're not staying at a resort that has a golf course, there are some fantastic public courses in the city.

All of the public courses listed here offer online booking through their websites. You can reserve a tee time online through one of these companies: **Golf Now** (Tel. 800/767-3574. www.golfnow.com) and **Stand-By Golf** (Tel. 760/321-2665. www.standbygolf.com).

Indian Canyons Golf Resort
Located in the south part of the city, this resort (*pictured above*) has two 18-hole championship courses. One of the courses is known for the Walt Disney Fountain, which shoots water 100 feet (30.5 meters) into the sky. The course is on tribal land, and the setting is spectacular. There's a pro shop, restaurant, and rental shop. *Info*: 1097 Murray Canyon Dr. Tel 760/833-8700. From $40. www.indiancanyonsgolf.com.

Tahquitz Creek Golf Course
This 18-hole regulation course dates back to 1957, and features desert landscaping, beautiful mountain views, and scenic waterscapes. There's a pro shop, bar, restaurant, rental shop, driving range, chipping green, and two large putting greens. *Info*: 1885 Golf Club Dr./Lawrence Crossley Rd. Tel 760/328-1005. From $59. www.tahquitzgolfresort.com.

Golfing

1. Escena
2. Indian Canyons
3. Tahquitz Creek

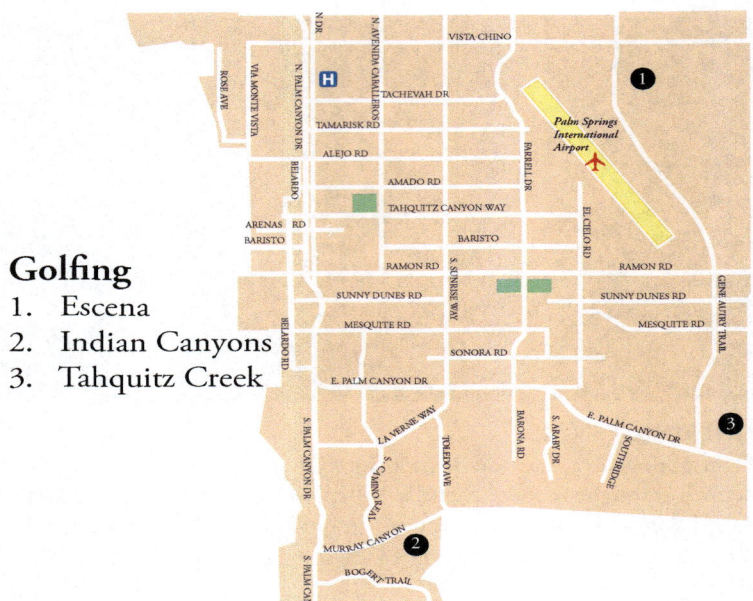

Escena Golf Club
The new kid on the block, Escena has an 18-hole course featuring desert landscaping and incredible mountain views. There's a restaurant (known for its weekend brunch), bar, and rental shop. *Info*: 1100 Clubhouse View Dr. Tel. 760/778-2737. From $90. www.escenagolf.com.

TENNIS/PICKLEBALL

The Coachella Valley is a huge destination for tennis players. In addition to the BNP Paribas Open held in March (*see next page*), there are many tennis-club resorts. Here are a few:
- Palm Springs Tennis Club, 701 W. Baristo Rd., Palm Springs. Tel. 760/318-1716. www.palmspringstennisclub.info.
- CC Tennis Club, 6831 Paseo Real, Cathedral City. Tel. 760/321-7467. cctennisclub.com.
- La Quinta Resort & Club, 49-499 Eisenhower Dr., La Quinta. Tel. 760/564-4111. laquintaresort.com.
- JW Marriott Desert Springs Resort, 74-855 Country Club Dr., Palm Desert. Tel. 760/341-2211. www.marriott.com.

PALM SPRINGS/COACHELLA VALLEY 53

FESTIVALS/EVENTS
BNP Paribas Open
This international tennis tournament is held in March at the fantastic Indian Wells Tennis Garden in Indian Wells. It's the first of nine ATP World Tour Masters tournaments, draws fans from around the world, and showcases the best players the sport has to offer. The main stadium seats over 16,000 spectators and is the second-largest in the world.

Info: 78-200 Miles Ave., Indian Wells. Tel. 760/200-8400. bnpparibasopen.com.

Coachella
For the past 20 years, the Coachella Valley Music and Arts Festival has been a destination for music lovers and trendsetters. Held on two weekends in April at the Empire Polo Club in Indio, it is one of the most renowned music festivals in the world.. Can you say Beyoncé?
Info: www.coachella.com.

Stagecoach
Country music fans have their own Coachella Valley Music Festival, Stagecoach, featuring the industry's top country artists. It's also held every April at the Empire Polo Club in Indio, and is one of the most popular country music events in the world. *Info*: www.stagecoachfestival.com.

LGBTQ+
Palm Springs has three events that draw thousands of LGBTQ+ visitors to the city every year. **Pride,** held the first weekend in November, includes a fun festival and a Sunday parade that attracts over 60,000 people.
www.pspride.info. **White Party** for gay men (www.whitepartyglobal.com) and **The Dinah** for lesbians (www.thedinah.com) take place every year.

Golf Tournament
Beginning in 1960, when Arnold Palmer won, **The Desert Classic PGA Tournament** is held at the PGA West's Jack Nicklaus Tournament Resort Course at the La Quinta Country Club. *Info*: www.laquintaresort.com and www.pgatour.com.

Modernism Week
Modernism Week is a celebration of mid-century modern design, architecture, fashion, art, and culture. The festival is held in February, and includes architectural walking and home tours, lectures, and (of course) festive cocktail parties. There's also the annual Palm Springs Modernism Show & Sale with world-class exhibitors. This is a huge event in the city, and has grown each year. Modernism Week has now added a fall preview in October. For a list of all the events, visit www.modernismweek.com.

Tour de Palm Springs
Every February, this event attracts thousands of novice to elite bike riders who bike from five to 100 miles (161 km) throughout the Coachella Valley, benefiting non-profit organizations. *Info*: www.tourdepalmsprings.com.

Festival of Lights
The Festival of Lights Parade along Palm Canyon Drive in downtown Palm Springs is an annual event in early December. Forget how cold you are (just kidding), and join 100,000 people who line the route to celebrate the holiday season. *Info*: www.psfestivaloflights.com.

Palm Desert Half Marathon
The Palm Desert Half Marathon and 5K takes place every February in and around Palm Desert, for both individual runners and relay teams. *Info*: www.palmdeserthalfmarathon.com.

PALM SPRINGS/COACHELLA VALLEY 55

Desert X
Contemporary art installations are displayed every other spring in the Coachella Valley. Thought-provoking works are featured throughout the desert. *Info*: Admission: Free. Locations can be found at desertx.org. *See photo above.*

Walk of the Inns
A wonderful evening in Palm Springs! This self-guided walking tour takes you through some of the most interesting and historic hotels downtown (where you just might hear a story or two about famous former guests). You'll start at the Palm Springs Art Museum at 101 Museum Drive—to get your complimentary admission and a free map and flashlight—then it's off to investigate! Participating hotels change every year, and have included Casa Cody, Coyote Inn, Desert Hills Resort, Del Marcos Hotel, Old Ranch Inn, Orbit Inn, Palm Mountain Resort & Spa, and the Viceroy Resort Hotel. It's really a fun night—but remember to wear comfy shoes! *Info*: www.visitpalmsprings.com.

Village Fest
This street fair is held in downtown Palm Springs every Thursday night along North Palm Canyon Drive. Arts, crafts, entertainment, and food. A great night for a stroll! (And if you feel like shopping, you're in luck: Many stores stay open late.) *Info*: villagefest.org.

Splash House

The ultimate pool party takes place three weekends each summer and is hosted by three hotels Palm Springs hotels. In past years it's been held at Saguaro, Renaissance, and Margaritaville. You buy a pass or hotel package that gives you admission to all resorts for the weekend. There's an additional charge to dance the night away after hours at the Palm Springs Air Museum. Shuttles run between all hotel venues and to the after-hours parties at the Air Museum. *Info*: General admission wristbands from $210. Tickets for the after-hours party from $60. www.splashhouse.com.

Tram Road Challenge

If you're looking for a fun, unique way to gasp for air, the Palm Springs Aerial Tram Road Challenge is a 3.7 mile (6 km), all-uphill run on the road leading up to the tram. And you don't need to run; many just walk. It takes place in late October when the temperatures have cooled off. *Info*: www.facebook.com/tramroadchallenge/.

COACHELLA VALLEY PRESERVE

This huge preserve has nearly 30 miles (48 km) of hiking trails through more than 13,000 acres of mountain and desert terrain. Several oases—among them the extraordinary Thousand Palm Oasis—are along the San Andreas Fault, where underground water rising to the desert surface created the perfect cool and damp environment for California fan palms to grow.

PALM SPRINGS/COACHELLA VALLEY 57

The interesting hike from the visitor center on the flat and easy McCallum Trail will take you to McCallum Pond at Thousand Palms Oasis (about 2 miles [3.2 km] round-trip). There are stops along the trail that describe the San Andreas Fault, fan palms, wildlife, and the geologic and ecologic features of the preserve. You'll pass through lush vegetation on raised wooden paths. After the oasis, the trail winds through a sandy wash before reaching McCallum Grove.

After leaving the grove, you can take the trail west. It's slightly uphill and will lead you to an overlook for great views of the area. From there you can extend the hike to the Moon Canyon Trail (about 4 miles [6.4 km]). *Info*: 29200 Thousand Palms Canyon Road. From Palm Springs take Ramon Road east to Thousand Palms Canyon Road and turn left. Guided hikes are available. Admission: Free (donations accepted). www.cnlm.org/portfolio_page/coachella-valley/.

Shields Date Farm
Do you like dates? They grow on trees—date palm trees, to be exact. And although they're native to the Middle East, huge groves can be found in California, too. In fact, the state accounts for over 90% of the country's total date production—grown mostly in the Coachella Valley, and south to the Mexican border. This date farm in Indio has a gift shop that offers free samples. And whatever you do, make sure you have a delicious date milkshake. There's a garden path that depicts 14 scenes of Christ's life, an interesting short film on the history of the date-farm industry, and a cafe where you can have date-flavored coffee. *Info*: 80-225 Highway 111, Indio. Tel. 760/347-0996. Open daily 9am-4pm. Admission: $5, under 13 free. www.shieldsdategarden.com.

DESERT HOT SPRINGS
Twelve miles (19 km) north of downtown Palm Springs.

In the 1950s, Desert Hot Springs (called "DHS" by locals) became a popular spa destination for its hot natural mineral springs.

One of the main attractions is **Cabot's Pueblo Museum**, a unique, Hopi-inspired structure created from reclaimed objects and materials. The massive building was begun by Cabot Yerxa in the late 1930s on property he homesteaded. He continued to work on the property until his death in 1965. Guided tours take visitors through the complex to learn about Yerxa's life and the items he collected. Of interest here is the 43-foot-tall "Waokiya" sculpture, carved from a giant cedar. *Info*: 67616 E. Desert View Ave. Tel. 760/329-7610. Open Oct-May Tue-Sun 9am-4pm, Jun-Sep Tue-Sat 9am-1pm. Admission: $13. Tour of the grounds: $5. www.cabotsmuseum.org.

There are many resorts and spas here. A few worth noting are:

El Morocco Inn & Spa $$
For a novel experience, relax in the hot natural mineral springs at this Moroccan-themed inn. Day-spa guests ($60 for a day pass) have access to the pool, spa, and two dry saunas. A locker, robe, and towel are provided, along with coffee, tea, water, and healthy snacks. (Hotel guests enjoy the nightly "Morocco-tini" hour.) *Info*: 66810 4th St. Tel. 760/288-2527. www.elmoroccoinn.com.

Spring Resort and Spa $$$
This small 12-room resort features three mineral pools, splendid mountain views, and a laid-back experience. Most rooms look out to the pool. The hotel also has a fire pit where guests can take in the stars while sipping on a beverage. *Info*: 12699 Reposo Way. Tel. 760/251-6700. www.the-spring.com.

Tuscan Springs Hotel & Spa $$
This Italian-inspired hotel offers rooms with either mountain or garden views. You can relax in two natural mineral water Jacuzzis and a large natural mineral water pool. The water is pumped from an aqua well that is volcanically heated to 115 degrees (46 C). There are only 16 room here, so this boutique hotel is quite quiet. Breakfast is included. *Info*: 68187 Club Circle. Tel. 760/251-0189. Day pass is $50 (for four hours). www.tuscansprings.com.

The Lautner Compound $$$
This complex, built in 1947, is named for John Lautner, a famous mid-century modern designer. The Lautner offers four luxury rental units, so guests enjoy their own private residence while having access to the amenities of a boutique hotel. Unique. *Info*: 67710 San Antonio St. Tel. 760/832-5288. www.thelautner.com.

Many of the hotels in the city have upscale restaurants. You'll also find some really good, authentic Mexican eateries.

South of the Border ($-$$) is one such spot (11719 Palms Dr., Tel. 760/251-4000. Open daily) and **Casa Blanca ($-$$)** is another (66370 Pierson Blvd. Tel. 760/251-5922. Open daily. www.casablancamenu.com).

3. Joshua Tree and the Hi-Desert

- Joshua Tree National Park
- Morongo Valley
- Yucca Valley
- Pioneertown
- Landers
- Joshua Tree
- Twentynine Palms
- Whitewater Preserve/ Sand to Snow National Monument

JOSHUA TREE/HI-DESERT 61

JOSHUA TREE NATIONAL PARK

Unique trees, rugged rock formations, desert cacti, and stark landscapes draw visitors to Joshua Tree. It's truly unforgettable—and it's an easy day trip from Palm Springs. The two could not be more different: While Palm Springs is stylish and trendy, Joshua Tree is bohemian and mystical. The northern part of the park is in the high-altitude Mojave Desert, while the southern portion is part of the Colorado Desert.

The region has been inhabited for at least 5,000 years, first by the Pinto Culture, then by Native American tribes including the Serrano, the Chemehuevi, and the Cahuilla. In the 1800s, cattlemen arrived; then miners looking for gold. You can still see the mines they abandoned throughout Joshua Tree.

The famous tree was named by early Mormon settlers after the Old Testament prophet Joshua, as its branches reminded them of Joshua raising his arms to pray. And Joshua trees aren't actually trees; they're succulents (plants that store water). Joshua trees (*yucca brevifolia*) grow very slowly, about two to three inches every year. It takes 50 to 60 years for one to reach full height, and they live, on average, for 500 years.

Almost three million people come to Joshua Tree each year—some just to see the riot of color when desert wildflowers bloom in spring. And, of course, there's always the powerful pull of the desert environment itself, as we mentioned earlier. But don't forget: this is a park, after all—and a massive one at that! Almost 800,000 acres for biking, hiking, horseback riding, rock climbing, camping, exploring...

There are several ways to enter the park: Yucca Valley in the west (Black-Rock Nature Center), Twentynine Palms in the north (Oasis Visitor Center), and Cottonwood Springs in the south (Cottonwood Visitor Center). The main Visitor Center in the town of Joshua Tree is on Park Boulevard, which will take you directly to Lost Horse Valley, in the heart of the park. From there, three short trails (Hidden Valley, Barker Dam, and Cap Rock) offer a great introduction to Joshua Tree.

Not everyone comes here to hike—especially in the summer, when the desert heat is downright dangerous. So drive! Park Boulevard (often crowded in high season) travels 25 miles (40 km) from the West Entrance in the town of Joshua Tree to the North Entrance in Twentynine Palms. (If you're coming from the Cottonwood Visitor Center in the south, it's a 50-mile (80.5 km) drive to the West Entrance.) Make sure your car has a full tank of gas and you have food and water, as there are no facilities in the park. And never forget you're in the desert—so cell-phone service isn't always reliable!

Major sights:
The **Oasis of Mara**, just outside the park boundary at Highway 62 and Utah Trail near the Oasis Visitor Center, would be a good place to start your visit. There's a paved nature trail looping through the oasis that's only a half-mile (.8 km) walk and accessible by wheelchair (a rarity in the park), with markers along the way highlighting the area's history.

JOSHUA TREE/HI-DESERT 63

Black Rock Canyon (Highway 247 at the northwest part of the park) is another good starting point. The popular Hi-View Nature Trail (1.3 miles [2 km]) here is lined with markers describing the plants and natural features you'll see along the way, and it's also the trailhead for the ambitious 36-mile (58 km) California Riding and Hiking Trail.

At **Hidden Valley** (on Park Boulevard 10 miles (16 km) south of the West Entrance), you'll be surrounded by massive (definitely *not* hidden!) boulders as you explore—including a meadow with markers describing the landscape here.

Skull Rock (Park Boulevard near Jumbo Rocks Campground) takes its name from the rock formation that looks like two hollow eyes. This area is a favorite of rock climbers, and the 1.7-mile (2.7 km) hike here is one of the most popular in the park.

Cap Rock (at the intersection of Park Boulevard and Keys View Road) is named after a flat, cap-like rock balanced on top of boulders. The easy trail is less than a half-mile (.8 km) round-trip. The country/rock singer Gram Parson's body was cremated here in 1973 by his friends to fulfill his wishes. (He had died in a Joshua Tree motel of a drug overdose.)

Keys View (Keys View Road) will provide you with the best views in the park. From its elevation at over 5,000 feet (1,524 meters), you can see Palm Springs, the Coachella Village, the San Andreas Fault, and (on clear days) the Salton Sea.

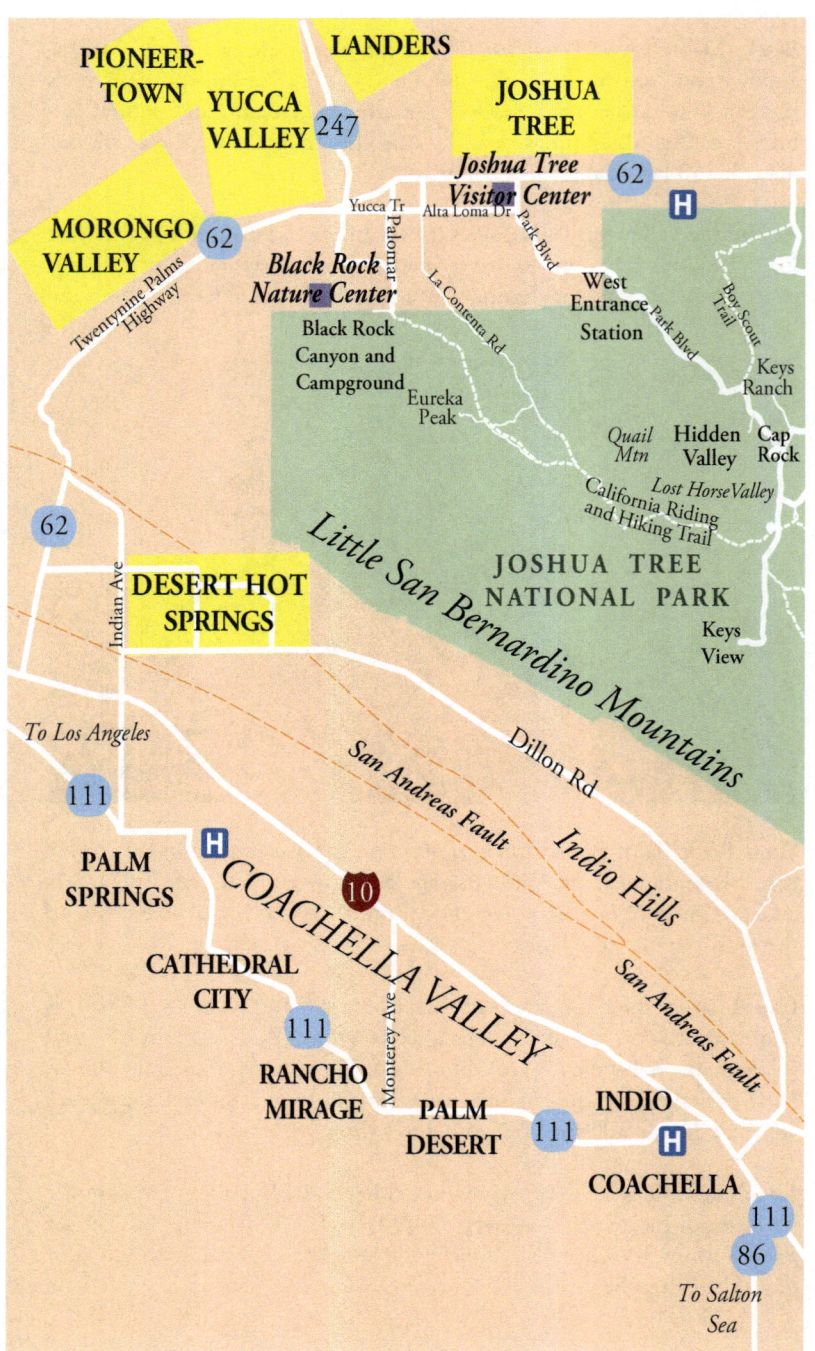

JOSHUA TREE/HI-DESERT 65

TWENTYNINE PALMS

To Marine Corps Center
Adobe Rd
Amboy Rd
To 40

Joshua Tree National Park Visitor Center
Oasis of Mara
Utah Trail
62

Fortynine Palms Oasis
Indian Cove
North Entrance Station
Twentynine Palms Mountains
Gold Crown Rd

Queen Mountain
Barker Dam
Park Blvd
Old Dale Mining District

Queen Valley
Bighorn Pass
Sheep Pass
Ryan Mtn
Skull Rock
Jumbo Rocks
Belle
White Tank

Pinto Mountains

Lost Horse Mine
Geology Tour Rd.
Wilson Canyon
Cholla Cactus Garden
Ocotillo Patch

Pleasant Valley
Hexie Mountains
Pinto Basin Rd
Old Dale Rd
Pinto Basin
Black Eagle Mine R

Berdoo Canyon

Monument Mountain

10 Miles
10 Kilometers
Hiking trails
Paved Roads

Pinkham Canyon
Thermal Canyon

Cottonwood Visitor Center
Cottonwood Spring

Eagle Mountain

Cottonwood Mountains
Lost Palms Oasis
Bajada Nature Trail

10
Box Cny Rd
10 *To Arizona*

To Salton Sea

Ocotillo Patch is located off Pinto Basin Road, where you'll be surrounded by plenty of ocotillos. This interesting plant is found throughout the desert. At times, it can look like a bunch of dead sticks; and at other times, it sprouts oval-shaped leaves and red flowers. Also here are palo verde trees, a desert tree with green branches and trunk.

The **Cholla Cactus Garden** is one of our favorite destinations in the park. It's 20 miles (32 km) north of the Cottonwood Visitors Center on Pinto Basin Road. Grab a pamphlet and learn about the cholla cactus and other cacti of the region. The "furry" cholla have the nickname "teddy bear." The spines are anything but soft, so be careful: they seem to jump off the cactus! Also here are pencil cholla, with long spines. The trail here is only a quarter of a mile (.4 km).

Cottonwood Springs: This oasis is located near the south Visitor Center. A steep three-mile (4.8 km) round-trip trail takes you from the spring to the Mastodon gold mine. This is one of the best places to experience the springtime bloom of desert wildflowers. And if you're up to it, the Lost Palms Oasis is the largest grove of fan palms in the park—but it's a difficult, eight-mile (12.8 km) round-trip hike.

JOSHUA TREE/HI-DESERT 67

Camping
There are 500 campsites in the park. Most campgrounds require online reservations at www.recreation.gov. They include Black Rock Canyon, Jumbo Rocks, Indian Cove, Cottonwood, and Ryan. Cost per night for Black Rock and Cottonwood is $25. Cost per night at Indian Cove, Jumbo Rocks, and Ryan is $20.

Some campgrounds are available on a first-come, first-served basis. They include: Hidden Valley, Belle, and White Tank. Cost per night is $15.

Only Black Rock and Cottonwood have drinking water and flush toilets. All other campgrounds have pit toilets. There are no RV hookups at any of the campgrounds, but Black Rock and Cottonwood have dump stations. All have fire grates and tables. Frequent fire bans are issued and prohibit both campfires and grill fires.

Make sure you check the website while planning your trip, as the need for reservations changes due to weather and availability.

Biking
You can bike here, but only on the paved and backcountry roads. And there are no bike-rental shops in the park, but you can rent a bike in the town of Joshua Tree at Joshua Tree Bicycle Shop. *Info*: 6416 Hallee Rd. Tel. 760/366-3377. Open Wed-Sat 10am-6pm. Closed Sun-Tue. From $65 per day. www.jtbikeshop.com.

Most bike along the main, paved road, Park Boulevard, which runs from the West Entrance in Joshua Tree to the North Entrance in Twentynine Palms (25 miles [40 km]). You'll find less traffic on Pinto Basin Road from the South Entrance at Cottonwood.

If you want to hit the dirt roads on a mountain bike, the two most popular routes are the Geology Tour Road (18 miles [29 km]) and Queen Valley (13 miles [21 km]).

Horseback Riding
To experience the park by horse, you can either bring your own, or rent from Knob Hill Ranch, located near the West Entrance. 57840 Cortez Dr., Yucca Valley. *Info*: Tel. 760/333-1771. Guided rides from $165. www.knobhillranch.com.

There are over 250 miles (402 km) of equestrian trails. The best known is the 36-mile (58 km) California Riding and Hiking Trail that runs from Black Rock Canyon to the North Entrance.

Rock Climbing
Rock climbers from all over the world head to Joshua Tree to tackle the incredible boulder formations. Mojave Guides offers rock climbing experiences at www.mojaveguides.com. The main rock-climbing destinations in the park include Hidden Valley, Cap Rock, Quail Springs, Wonderland Wash, Intersection Rock, Split Rock, and Conan's Corridor.

Pets
Park regulations do not allow pets to join you on hiking trails, in the backcountry, or in park buildings.

JOSHUA TREE/HI-DESERT 69

How to get to Joshua Tree
From Palm Springs: To the West and North entrances, take I-10 west to California Route 62 (Twentynine Palms Highway) to Twentynine Palms (40 miles/64 km).
From Los Angeles: To the West and North entrances, take I-10 east to California Route 62 (Twentynine Palms Highway) to Twentynine Palms (140 miles/225 km).
From Indio: The South Entrance is located at Cottonwood Spring, approximately 25 miles (40 km) east of Indio off I-10.

When to Visit
Joshua Tree National Park is open year-round. The best time to visit is in spring and fall, when high temperatures average 85°F (29°C) and lows around 50°F (10°C). Winter brings cool temperatures, around 60°F (15°C), and nights that can dip below freezing. In winter, it snows in higher elevations. Summers are brutally hot, with temperatures often above 100°F (38°C). The Mojave Desert in the park's northern part is slightly cooler than the Colorado Desert in the southern part of the park.

Practical Information
Joshua Tree Visitor Center (6554 Park Blvd., Joshua Tree) is open daily 7:30am-5pm. Joshua Tree National Park Visitor Center (6533 Freedom Way, Twentynine Palms) is open daily 8:30am-5pm. Cottonwood Visitor Center (Pinto Basin Road, seven miles [11 km] north of I-10, Exit 168) is open daily 8:30am-4pm. Black Rock Nature Center (9800 Black Rock Canyon Rd., Yucca Valley) is open daily 8am-11am and noon-4pm with limited hours in the summer. The telephone number for all centers is 760/367-5500.

Entrance fee per vehicle is $30, motorcycles $25, individuals on foot or bicycle $15. All entrance fees are good for a consecutive period of seven days. Annual passes are $55.

For up-to-date news on Joshua Tree, visit www.nps.gov/jotr.

HI-DESERT TOWNS

The Hi-Desert (High Desert) towns along the northern border of the national park provide a gateway to the park. Each has its own identity, and we'll explore them here. To reach the Hi-Desert from Palm Springs, take N. Indian Canyon Dr. to California Highway 62. The distance to the town of Joshua Tree is 35 miles (56 km).

Morongo Valley
21 miles (34 km) west of the park's West Entrance.

Most travelers pass this residential community on their way to Joshua Tree. There are a few eateries, bars, and a gas station (you should think about fueling up, as there are no facilities in the park). You might find the **Cactus Mart** worth a stop. Not only can you check out the cacti and succulents, but there's a shop selling coffee, pottery, and works by local artists. They also have a good selection of books focusing on hiking and plants. *Info*: 49889 Twentynine Palms Highway. Tel. 760/363-6076. Open daily 9am-5pm. www.cactusmart.com. Also here is **Black Luck**, a vintage shop with interesting clothing and household goods. *Info*: 49950 Twentynine Palms Highway, Tel. 760/418-4514. Open Thu-Mon 10am-5pm.

Eating & Drinking in Morongo Valley
Spaghetti Western Saloon $$
A Spaghetti Western is a low-budget film produced by Italian directors and filmed in Europe. This restaurant in Morongo Valley is owned and operated by Italian transplants, Jasmine and Lorenzo Tomasso. Start with bruschetta (toasted bread, tomatoes, mozzarella, basil, and balsamic drizzle). The specialty pasta here is Spaghetti Western (smoked pepper bacon, tomato sauce, and pecorino cheese). One of the featured cocktails is the Redwood Rattlesnake (Redwood Empire rye whiskey, maple syrup, bitters, and an orange peel). A welcome addition to Hi-Desert dining. *Info*: 50048 Twentynine Palms Highway, Morongo Valley. Tel. 760/363-7444. Open Thu-Sun 5pm-10pm. www.spaghettiwesternsaloon.com.

JOSHUA TREE/HI-DESERT

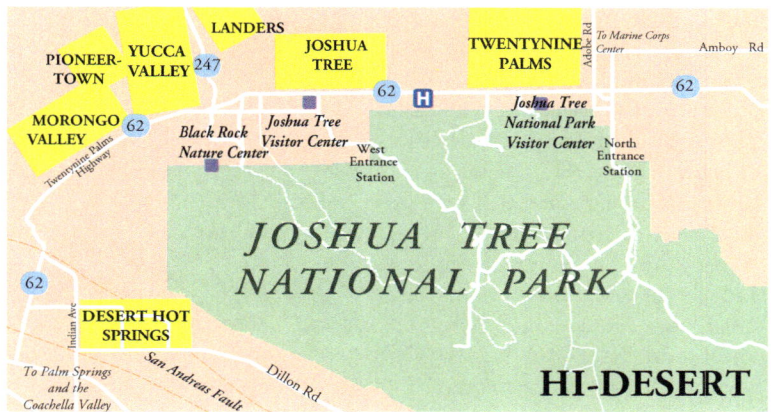

Yucca Valley
13 miles (21 km) west of the park's West Entrance.

There are plenty of national stores in the strip malls here, but most shoppers are drawn to the vintage clothing stores, antique shops, and funky boutiques. All the shops are within easy walking distance of each other.

For vintage clothing and accessories, head to **The End**. *Info*: 55872 Twentynine Palms Highway. Tel. 760/418-5536. Open daily 11am-5pm. www.theendyuccavalley.com. If you want to check out bohemian and mid-century modern home-decor items, visit **Acme 5 Lifestyle**. *Info*: 55870 Twentynine Palms Highway. Tel. 760/853-0031. Open daily 11am-5pm. www.acme5lifestyle.com. Everything hip (clothing, boots, housewares, jewelry, and art) is stocked at the fun **Hoof and the Horn**. *Info*: 55840 Twentyninepalms Highway. Tel. 760/365-6100. Open daily 11am-6pm. www.hoofandthehorn.com.

Art, pottery, and antiques from several vendors are at **Pioneer Crossing Antiques**. *Info*: 55854 Twentynine Palms Highway. Tel. 760/228-0603. Open Fri-Mon 10am-5pm. www.pioneercrossingantiques.com. More antiques are found at **Route 62 Vintage Marketplace**. *Info*: 55635 Twentynine Palms Highway. Tel. 760/365-4430. Open daily 10am-4pm.

If you are in Yucca Valley on a Saturday or Sunday morning, think about visiting a flea market. This is one mess of a place, but we love it. **The Sky Village Swap Meet** has lots of junk, but also some Western ware. Buried in the flea market is the curious "cave" of crystals. Walk through it, peer through the small windows, and get groovy. They even have a small diner at the market. *Info*: 7028 Theatre Rd. Tel. 760/365-2105. Open Sat 6am-2pm and Sun 7am-2pm. www.skyvillageswapmeet.com.

Eating & Drinking in Yucca Valley

Hungry? Coffee, breakfast, brunch, and lunch are offered at both **C&S Coffee Shop** (55795 Twentynine Palms Highway. Tel. 760/365-9946. Open daily) and **Frontier Cafe** (55844 Twentynine Palms Highway. Tel. 760/820-1360. Open daily 7am-5pm. www.cafefrontier.com).

Tiny Pony $$

This restaurant in a strip mall was once a gun shop and a beauty salon. It's now a welcoming and quirky eatery in Yucca Valley. The owners call their menu "elevated bar food." You'll find everything from burgers to steak to cast iron scallops on the menu. And the drink menu includes interesting concoctions like the Pickletini, made with gin, pickle juice, and celery. A decent list of natural wines adds to the experience. The LGBTQ+ community is openly welcomed at this wonderful addition to Hi-Desert dining. *Info*: 7205 Twentynine Palms Highway, Yucca Valley. Tel. (442) 205-0163. Open daily at 11am (Sat and Sun at 9am). www.thetinypony.com.

The Copper Room $$

Our favorite place to dine in Yucca Valley has been open since 1957. This restaurant and lounge overlooks the small Yucca Valley Airport. You'll feel you have stepped back in time. They offer shareable plates such as sesame long beans and marinated cucumbers along with main dishes like grilled steak, seared tofu sandwich, and hamburger with fries. Wash it all down with classic cocktails and ice cold martinis. Fun and fabulous! *Info*: 57360 Aviation Dr., Yucca Valley. Open Mon-Thu 4pm-10pm, Fri 4pm-midnight, Sat noon-midnight, Sun noon-10pm. thecopperroom1957.com.

JOSHUA TREE/HI-DESERT 73

Pioneertown
Five miles (8 km) north of Yucca Valley (turn left onto Pioneertown Rd. from Route 62).

If you feel like you're on a movie set in Pioneertown, it's because you are. In the 1940s, a group of investors and filmmakers built an "Old West" town here—including a saloon, jail, bank, chapel, and stables—that was also a modern town, with modern-day conveniences and entertainment—like grocery stores, motels, bowling alleys, and bars—where cowboy stars like Roy Rogers and Gene Autry could relax after a day of shooting (pun intended). During its heyday, hundreds of movies and TV shows were filmed here, and the town flourished. But when Westerns fell out of favor, so did Pioneertown. Happily, it's a popular tourist destination once again—both for visitors to nearby Joshua Tree National Park, and in its own right.

This wild-west town is worth a stroll, but it's **Pappy & Harriet's Pioneertown Palace** that draws most people. Some of the famous visitors who have performed here include Paul McCartney, Robert Plant, Rufus Wainwright, Lucinda Williams, Leon Russell, Daniel Lanois, Wanda Jackson, Ricki Lee Jones, Lorde, and Ke$ha. The food served here includes ribs, burgers, sandwiches, and salads. *Info*: 53688 Pioneertown Rd. Tel. 760/228-2222. Open Thu and Fri 11am-11pm, Sat and Sun 10am-11pm, Mon 4pm-11pm. Closed Tue and Wed. No reservations. www.pappyandharriets.com.

The rustic 20-room **Pioneertown Motel** has been updated, and you can relax under the desert skies at one of the fire pits and hammocks. It's located within walking distance of Pappy & Harriet's. *Info*: 5240 Curtis Rd. Tel. 760/365-7001. From $230 per night. www.pioneertown-motel.com.

Landers

15 miles (24 km) north of Highway 62 on Highway 247 (Old Woman Springs Road).

Where? Even those of us who live in the area aren't terribly familiar with this small town. Landers has drawn visitors for very different reasons.

One interesting destination is the **Integratron**. Aeronautical engineer George Van Tassel was obsessed with UFOs. He built this dome structure after he claimed that extraterrestrials from Venus gave him the blueprint. He wanted the dome to promote time travel and be an "electrostatic generator." Today you can reserve a spot to have a sound bath, to relax and rejuvenate. If taking a break from your life and listening to the music of crystal bowls appeals to you, then this is the ticket. *Info*: 2477 Belfield Blvd. Tel. 760/364-3126. Reservations required. Admission: From $55. www.integratron.com.

Gubler Orchids

Heinrich Gubler began growing orchids in Switzerland in 1918. Moving to the U.S., his son Hans started Gubler Orchids in 1956—selling them out of his car. And today, orchids are still the family's passion—and business is blooming! *Info*: 2200 Belfield Blvd. Tel. 760/364-2282. Open Wed-Sat 10am-3:30pm. Closed holidays. Greenhouse tours $5 (no open-toe shoes). www.gublers.com.

What was once the largest freestanding boulder in the world (until a large section inexplicably broke off in 2000) is nearby at the aptly named **Giant Rock**. At seven stories tall, this huge rock is located on sacred Native American land. This is a destination for believers in UFOs, and unfortunately it's been marred by graffiti. You can reach Giant Rock from the Integratron by taking a right on Belfield Road for three miles (4.8 km) on a dirt road. *See photo on next page.*

The place to dine here is the surprising **La Copine**. This small restaurant has modern black-and-white décor and an interesting menu. Locals and visitors alike dine on dishes such as Salade Copine (featuring smoked salmon), crispy blackened chicken with cheesy grits, and cinnamon beignets. There's also a beer and wine selection. *Info*: 848 Old Woman Springs Rd., Flamingo Heights (10 miles [16 km] north of Yucca Valley). Tel. 760/289-8537. Hours and days open vary. Closed mid-Jun to Aug. lacopinekitchen.com. Moderate.

CONCERTS IN THE DESERT
Outdoor drive-in concerts are held at a 15-acre ranch in Yucca Valley. This unique experience lets you relax under the stars while performers entertain you from a stage under a large Joshua tree. Bring some chairs, snacks, and a bottle of wine! The concerts are free, but you must RSVP. Donations appreciated. *Info*: 57050 Sun Mesa Dr., Yucca Valley. www.monpetitmojave.com

Joshua Tree
Seven miles (11 km) east of Yucca Valley.

Lots of people stop in this laid-back town on their way to and from the national park, so you'll find plenty of welcoming hotels, restaurants, gift shops, and boutiques.

Shopping in Joshua Tree
Coyote Corner, a fun, touristy shop near the entry of the national park, has got you covered: souvenirs, hiking gear, camping supplies, T-shirts, and locally made jewelry. *Info*: 6535 Park Blvd. Tel. 760/366-9683. Open daily 9am-6pm. www.jtcoyotecorner.com.

Vintage clothing and accessories can be found at **Ricochet Vintage Wears**. It's known for recycled cowgirl and cowboy boots and shirts. *Info*: 61731 Twentynine Palms Highway. Tel. 760/366-1898. Open Mon 10am-1pm, Thu-Sun 10am-4pm. Closed Tue and Wed. www.ricochetjoshuatree.com.

Jen Rossi sells women's clothing (you need a kaftan, right?) at **Jen's Pirate Booty**. *Info*: 61729 Twentynine Palms Highway. Tel. 760/974-9800. Open daily 10am-5pm. www.jenspiratebooty.com.

Our favorite store is **The Station** (located in an old gas station) selling vintage and new items, along with gifts and fun T-shirts. Take a photo with "Josh," the giant cowboy statue, which was originally in the Salton Sea area. You can also relax with a cup of coffee or cold drink. *Info*: 61943 Twentynine Palms Highway. Tel. 760/974-9050. Open Sun and Mon 10am-5pm, Thu-Sat 10am-6pm. Closed Tue and Wed. www.thestationjoshuatree.com.

Eating in Joshua Tree
Crossroads Café ($-$$) is popular with locals and visitors. You can't miss its brick and rusted corrugated tin facade. This cafe serves comfort food with many vegan and vegetarian options. Dinner is a laid-back affair with a beer and wine selection. Try the Dirt Bag, a chicken and cilantro soup served over a biscuit. *Info*: 61715 Twentynine Palms Highway. Tel. 760/366-5414. Open daily. www.crossroadscafejtree.com.

Joshua Tree Saloon ($-$$) is a bar and grill that serves good burgers, sandwiches, and salads. Its outdoor patio, The Yard, is a popular place to hang out on weekends (featuring live music on many nights). Try the fish tacos in both grilled and fried cod. *Info*: 61835 Twentynine Palms Highway. Tel. 760/366-2250. Open daily at 10am. www.joshuatreesaloon.com.

Sleeping in Joshua Tree
Mojave Sands $$
Built in the 1950s, this funky renovated motel features a large koi pond and desert landscaping. There are three rooms, two suites, and five "luxury" rooms. Each unit has a private patio, walk-in shower, refrigerator, and a record player with an assortment of vinyl records. The suites also have small kitchenettes. *Info*: 62121 Twentynine Palms Highway. Tel. 760/550-8063. www.mojavesandsatjoshuatree.com.

Joshua Tree Inn $$
Singer/songwriter Gram Parsons spent his last days here and there's a shrine to him. The 11-room inn was built in 1949 in the Spanish Colonial style. Spanish-tiled courtyard rooms surround the pool, and there's a fire pit to hang around at night. *Info*: 61259 Twentynine Palms Highway. Tel. 760/366-1188. www.joshuatreeinn.com.

Safari $
This motor inn is the budget choice in Joshua Tree. There's a pool, and rooms have coffee makers and small refrigerators. Convenient location to the national park, and downtown shops and restaurants. *Info*: 61959 Twentynine Palms Highway. Tel. 760/366-1113. www.joshuatreemotel.com.

Twentynine Palms
15 miles (24 km) east of Joshua Tree.

Twentynine Palms is greatly influenced by the military base located here. Spread out over the desert, this small town is another gateway to Joshua Tree National Park. The Visitor Center here is not as busy as the main center at Joshua Tree.

JOSHUA TREE/HI-DESERT

Like other Hi-Desert towns, artists have moved in, and there are a couple of galleries featuring the works of locals, including **Twentynine Palms Creative Center and Gallery** (6847 Adobe Rd. Tel. 760/361-3461. Closed Mon and Sun. www.29palmsart.com) and **Twentynine Palms Art Gallery and Artist Guild** (74055 Cottonwood Dr. Tel. 760/367-7819. Open Fri-Sun 11am-3pm. www.29palmsartgallery.com).

If you're hungry, head to **Kitchen in the Desert** ($$). This restaurant serves Caribbean and New American food, and is conveniently situated just outside the Twentynine Palms entrance to Joshua Tree National Park.

The menu includes jerk chicken, burgers, fried chicken sandwiches, with vegan and vegetarian options. There's no alcohol served, but you can BYOB. *Info*: 6427 Mesquite Ave. Tel. 760/865-0245. Open daily at 7am. www.kitcheninthedesert.com.

The place to eat and sleep here is the **29 Palms Inn** ($$). Family owned and operated for five generations, since 1928, this inn is located on 70 acres. You'll stay in a 1920s wood-frame cabin, a 1930s adobe bungalow, or a 1950s guest house. The poolside restaurant specializes in seafood, steaks, fish, and pasta specials (with vegetarian options). Sourdough bread is baked daily on the premises. *Info*: 73950 Inn Ave. Tel. 760/367-3505. 29palmsinn.com. Restaurant open Wed-Sun 2pm-8pm. Closed Mon and Tue.

WHITEWATER PRESERVE (SAND TO SNOW NATIONAL MONUMENT)
From the sands of the desert to the snowy San Gorgonio Peak (11,500 feet [3,505 meters]), the Sand to Snow National Monument offers an introduction to California's diverse topography.

Established as a national monument in the last decade, the Whitewater Preserve (a part of the Sand to Snow National Monument) is an easy day

trip from Palm Springs. From the stark desert to lush mountain greenery, the canyon is unlike any other area in Southern California. The visitors center here is located in the headquarters of the Whitewater Trout Farm (the former owner of the land). The Whitewater River is fed by mountain-snow melt and the preserve is subject to flash flooding, so check the website before visiting.

The **Canyon View Loop** is a great introduction to this unique destination. This 3.5-mile (6 km) loop begins at the ranger station and the main parking area, and there's a large rock listing the trails and their distances. You'll have splendid mountain and river views as you wander along the hike.

Also here is the **Red Dome Trail**. This four-mile (6.4 km) trek from the visitors center takes you to the incredible Pacific Crest Trail (a trail system that travels 2,600 miles [4,184 km] from Mexico to Canada).

The lovely **Whitewater-Mission Creek Trail** is a 6.5-mile (10.5 km) round-trip hike that starts with a two-mile (3.2 km) stretch of the Red Dome Trail.

Info: To reach Whitewater Preserve from Palm Springs, take N. Indian Canyon Dr. to I-10 West. Use exit 114. Follow Tipton Road to Whitewater Canyon Road for five miles (8 kilometers) to the entrance. Distance: 16 miles (26 kilometers). Tel. 760/325-7222. Admission: Free. www.wildlandsconservancy.org. Check the website before visiting as the preserve may be closed because of weather.

4. Excursions

- Cabazon
- Salton Sea
- Slab City/East Jesus
- Salvation Mountain
- Idyllwild
- Big Bear

CABAZON
From Palm Springs: 17 miles (27 km) on I-10 West toward Los Angeles (exit 106).

Cabazon Dinosaurs
This quirky attraction off I-10 as you approach Palm Springs from Los Angeles is a fun excursion, especially for kids. Two enormous steel-and-concrete dinosaurs are named Dinny the Dinosaur and Mr. Rex. These roadside dinosaurs are best known for their appearance in the mid-1980s film *Pee-wee's Big Adventure* and the music video *Everybody Wants To Rule The World* by Tears for Fears.

In 1964, theme-park artist Claude Bell began construction of the dinosaurs to draw more customers to a restaurant he had on the premises. Dinny and Mr. Rex were both created from material salvaged from the construction of I-10 and covered with spray concrete. Dinny was the first dinosaur to be used as a building. Today you can climb inside and take in the desert landscape. The World's Biggest Dinosaurs Museum here includes 70 robotic dinosaurs, a dinosaur garden, and the Wafflesaurus Truck serving snacks and ice cream on weekends. You can get pretty close to the dinosaurs to take photos, but you must pay to enter the museum, and to climb into the structures. *Info*: 50770 Seminole Dr., Cabazon. Tel. 909/272-8164. Open daily 9am-7pm. Closed Christmas. Admission: $15, ages 3-12 $13. www.cabazondinosaurs.com.

EXCURSIONS 83

Desert Hills Premium Outlets
This is one of the largest luxury outlets in California, with 180 designer and chain shops (Gucci, Armani, and The Gap). A bargain shopper's paradise, thousands visit this popular outdoor mall when they need a break from lounging around poolside in Palm Springs! *Info*: 48400 Seminole Dr., Cabazon. Open daily 10am-8pm.
www.premiumoutlets.com/outlet/desert-hills.

Morongo Casino Resort and Spa
You can't miss this huge casino and hotel if you're arriving from Los Angeles on Interstate 10. Located 18 miles (29 km) west of Palm Springs, it's a little bit of Las Vegas in the California desert. There's a bowling center, plenty of dining options, and a golf club. *Info*: 49500 Seminole Dr., Cabazon. Tel. 951/849-3080. www.morongocasinoresort.com.

SALTON SEA
From Palm Springs take I-10 east for 25 miles (40 km). Exit on Highway 86. To reach Bombay Beach and Niland on the east side of the Salton Sea, take Highway 111. To reach Salton City on the west side of the Salton Sea, take Route 86.

The Salton Sea isn't a sea at all; it's a lake—and an accidental one at that. Located in the Imperial Valley—one of California's most productive agricultural areas—it's the largest lake in the state, at 375 square miles (970 square km); one of the world's largest inland seas; and, at 227 feet (69 meters) below sea level, among the lowest spots on earth.

So, how did the lake end up in the desert? Here's the story: The Alamo Canal was built in 1901, to irrigate the Imperial Valley—part of the Salton Basin—with water from the Colorado River. But heavy rainfall and snowmelt in 1905 created a "perfect storm" of a chain reaction: the river swelled, causing the canal gates to break, causing a massive flood. Hello, Salton Sea!

In the 1950s and 1960s the Salton Sea became a popular tourist destination. Millions came to enjoy the warm water and the mountains, and towns like Salton City thrived. Frank Sinatra, Jerry Lewis, and other celebrities partied here; some no doubt at the nautically themed North Shore Beach & Yacht Club, designed by famous mid-century modern architect Albert Frey.

By the 1970s, rising salt levels—twice as salty as the Pacific Ocean—and fertilizer runoff created unsafe algae blooms and bacterial levels, with only a small amount of fresh water flowing in. This created a major environmental problem. Fish started to die off. In fact, so many died that former sandy beaches are now lined with fish bones; and at times during the year, the stench of decaying vegetation and dead fish can be overwhelming.

The area has an otherworldly look. Abandoned hotels and homes far outnumber those that are still occupied by the few remaining residents, and the dilapidated towns of Salton City and Bombay Beach look eerie. Many have said that the area looks like the set of a post-apocalyptic film.

And yet, the region still draws the curious traveler—even if it's just to photograph the fading billboards of the forgotten playground.

The area is a destination for birdwatchers, as birds use the lake as a migratory stopover. It's also the home of the **Sonny Bono Salton Sea National Wildlife Refuge**. The refuge was established as a sanctuary and breeding ground for birds and wild animals in 1930, and was renamed for former Congressman Sonny Bono, who advocated saving the Salton Sea. *Info*: www.fws.gov/refuge/sonny-bono-salton-sea.

The **Salton Sea Visitor Center** at the Salton Sea Recreation Area is located at 100-225 State Park Road, Mecca (near North Shore) off Highway 111. Tel. 760/393-3052. Open daily 10am-4pm.

EXCURSIONS 85

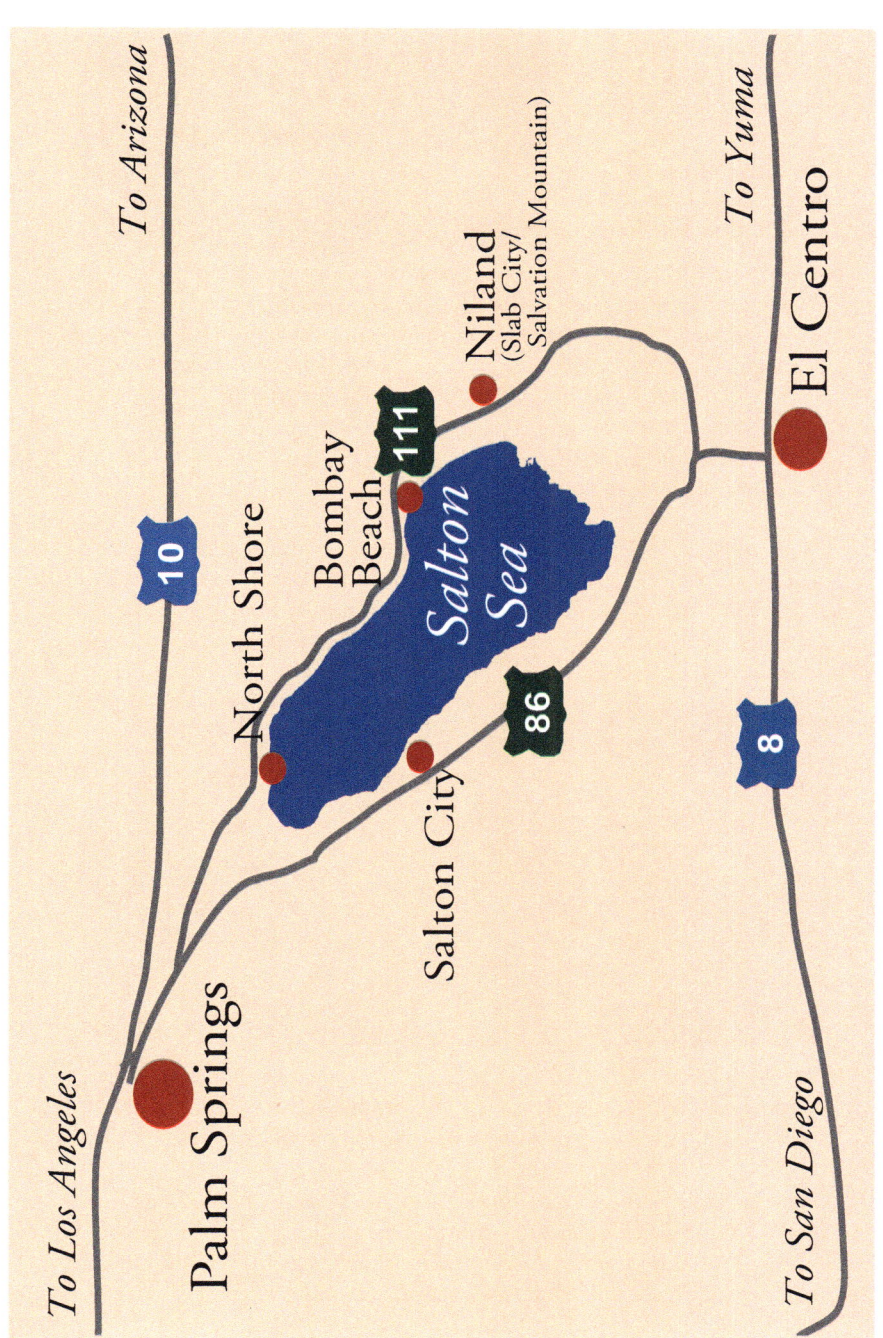

86 PALM SPRINGS MADE EASY

If you're looking for a place to eat and drink, there aren't many here.

The **Ski Inn**, with its retro sign, can be found in the town of Bombay Beach.

At 223 feet (68 meters) below sea level, it claims to be the lowest bar in the Western Hemisphere. The bar food is good and the beer cold, which you'll definitely want when temperatures climb way above 100 degrees F (38 degrees C). *Info*: 9596 Avenue A. Tel. 760/354-1285. Open Mon-Sat 10am-11pm, Sun 9am-9pm. Cash only. skiinn.business.site.

SLAB CITY/EAST JESUS
Just outside the town of Niland.

Slab City is a squatter community of people living off the grid in an assortment of recreational vehicles on a former Marine base. And if you're a fan of outsider art (and the people who create it), nearby East Jesus just might leave you speechless. *Info*: The Art Garden is open daily, sunrise to sunset. Admission: Free. eastjesus.org.

SALVATION MOUNTAIN
In the town of Niland near Slab City. From Highway 111, turn east on Main Street (which turns into Beal Road) and drive three miles (4.8 km).

Cement, adobe, and acres of junk: Leonard Knight's monument to redemption (including a painted "yellow brick road" to the cross at the top) is outsider art—pure and not-so-simple. You'll just have to see it (and maybe you still won't believe it). *Info*: www.salvationmountain.org.

IDYLLWILD
From Palm Springs there are two ways to get here. From Highway 111 (in Palm Desert) exit on Highway 74 to Highway 243 (41 miles [66 km]). You can also take Highway 111 from Palm Springs north to I-10 West to Banning. Exit onto Highway 243 for 25 miles (40 km).

We love this small town nestled above Palm Springs in the San Jacinto Mountains. Idyllwild (along with Pine Cove and Fern Valley) is a great day trip from Palm Springs, especially in the summer when you want to get away from the brutal heat.

The big draw here is the **San Jacinto National Park**, where you can hike over 50 trails surrounded by rocky outcroppings, cedars, and pines. The quaint town has locally owned restaurants and shops and somehow avoids the touristy vibe. Many artists have set up shop here, whose works are carried in Idyllwild's galleries and stores.

One of the popular shops here is **Nomad Ventures**, where you can shop for all your hiking, climbing, and backpacking needs. *Info*: 54415 N. Circle Dr. Tel. 951/659-4853. Open daily 9am-5pm. www.nomadventures.com.

You'll find plenty of short-term rentals in and around the town. One locally owned rental company with a large selection is **Idyllwild Vacation Cabins**. *Info*: 54380 N. Circle Dr. Tel 951/663-0527. www.idyllwildvacationcabins.com.

There are many hotels, motels, and camping facilities in town. A few include:

Idyllwild Inn $$
The historic family-owned inn has been around since 1904. It's located on over five acres within walking distance of the town center. Cabins, suites, and rooms have their own private decks. Most have fireplaces and kitchenettes. The newer suites even have hot tubs. *Info*: 54300 Village Center Dr. Tel. 951/659-2552. www.idyllwildinn.com.

Idyllwild Bunkhouse $$
This hotel/motel is located a mile (1.6 km) north of town. You'll find knotty pine interiors and a camping theme throughout. Several room options are available, and all have a kitchenette, Wi-Fi, and a television. A bonus is the breakfast delivered to your room every morning. *Info*: 25525 Highway 243. Tel. 951/659-2201. www.idyllwildbunkhouse.com.

The Grand Idyllwild Lodge $$$
This boutique craftsman-style lodge is nestled among the trees on over two acres of land, and offers superb mountain views from your room. There are ten suites and a villa. There's also a gym, sauna, and spa. This is your luxury choice in the area. *Info*: 54820 Pinecrest Ave. Tel. 951/659-2383. www.grandidyllwildlodge.com.

Idyllwild Campground $
Located in the Mount San Jacinto State Park, this year-round campground has 33 sites, and offers water, flush toilets, showers, and fire rings. It's within walking distance of the town center. *Info*: 25905 Highway 243. Tel. 951/659-2607. www.parks.ca.gov and www.reservecalifornia.com.

There are plenty of other campgrounds throughout the area. Most can be reserved at www.recreation.gov.

Idyllwild has great options for dining, especially in the town center. Here are a few:

Idyllwild Brewpub $$
Hand-crafted beer (especially the Idyllwild IPA), specialty cocktails, small plates, and main dishes (great burgers) are found at this lively place in the village center. Try the bison-sausage sandwich, or vegan stout chili. Dine inside or outside on the patio. *Info*: 54423 Village Center Dr. Tel. 951/659-0163. Open daily. www.idyllwildbrewpub.com.

Ferro $$-$$$
Indoor and outdoor seating at this favorite Italian restaurant. Plenty of pasta dishes to choose from. Try the *pollo arrosto* (citrus-brined free-range chicken) or *branzino con limone* (pan-roasted sea bass). The outdoor pizza oven lets you get an up-close look at your order (and is a comfortable seat on chilly nights). *Info*: 25840 Cedar St. Tel. 951/659-0700. Open daily. www.ferrorestaurant.com.

Gastrognome $$-$$$
Open since 1973, this is a favorite of locals and tourists. Friendly service, with three dining areas: indoor seating, the cafe, or the dog-friendly outdoor deck. Among your choices are pasta dishes, grilled trout, roast chicken, and plenty of steak options. Good wine list. *Info*: 54381 Ridgeview Dr. Tel. 951/659-5055. Closed Tue and Wed. www.gastrognome.com.

Tommy's Kitchen $$
Swiss-infused cuisine is served inside or outside on the shaded deck. Besides salads and sandwiches, you can try the hearty *sennen rosti* (Swiss hash browns with sauteed onions, ham, bacon, melted Swiss cheese, and two eggs). Brunch buffet or champagne brunch on Saturdays and Sundays. *Info*: 54700 N. Circle Dr. Tel. 951/468-4200. Closed Mon and Tue. www.tommyskitchenidyllwild.com. *Currently closed due to family health issues. Check the website before visiting.*

BIG BEAR

Big Bear is an outdoor-lover's dream. In winter, you can ski in Big Bear and then soothe your muscles in the hot tub in Palm Springs the same day. We've done it! In summer, you can escape the desert heat and hike or fish at Big Bear Lake. If you want to ski, there are plenty of ski-rental shops; and Big Bear Lake has two resorts: Snow Summit has 31 runs on 240 skiable acres; and Bear Mountain popular for snowboarding, with Southern California's only superpipe. There are also plenty of dining and sleeping options. Big Bear is 82 miles (132 km) by car from Palm Springs (following the I-10 West route).
www.bigbearmountainresort.com

5. Sleeping and Eating

SLEEPING
Short-Term Vacation Rentals
Many visitors to Palm Springs rent a home or condo through short-term rental sites. The city has very strict guidelines on short-term rentals, including heavy fines for violating the rules (like playing music). There are many local companies that offer a wide range of rental options. A few of them are:
- Altamira *www.altamirarentals.com.*
- Desert Luxury Estates *www.desertluxuryestates.com.*
- Luxsy *www.luxsypalmsprings.com.*
- Stay Poppy *www.staypoppy.com.*
- Palm Springs Rentals *www.palmspringsrentals.com.*
- Vacation Palm Springs *www.vacationpalmsprings.com.*

Sleeping Prices

Prices for two people in a double room:
- Expensive: over $200
- Moderate: $100-200
- Inexpensive: under $100

Hotels
North/Uptown/Movie Colony
ARRIVE $$-$$$
On the northern end of town is this groovy hotel with a butterfly roofline. There are 32 rooms, all with patios. Great pool scene for drinks and hanging out. Snacks are served poolside, and there's also a coffee shop and an ice cream parlor on the premises. **Palm Springs Swim & Social** serves all-day brunch at the pool. *Info*: 1551 N. Palm Canyon Dr. Tel. 760/507-1645. www.arrivehotels.com.

Alcazar $$

A boutique Spanish-Colonial hotel with a great location in the fun Uptown Design District. Chill on the private patio of one of the 34 rooms here, or relax at the pool or hot tub. The adjoining popular restaurants **Birba** and **Cheeky's** won't disappoint. *Info*: 622 Palm Canyon Dr. Tel. 760/318-9850. www.alcazarpalmsprings.com.

The Cole Hotel $$

The Cole opened in 2020 in the former Bahama Inn. Colorful, fresh, and fun, this mid-century modern hotel on the north end of town is a wonderful addition to the city. There are thirty guest rooms, a cafe, an indoor/outdoor bar, and a pool with cabanas and firepits. The hotel is also home to the excellent French restaurant, **Freddy's Kitchen**. *Info*: 2323 N. Palm Canyon Dr. Tel. 617/300-0356. www.sonder.com.

Colony Palms $$-$$$

This iconic hotel in the Movie Colony neighborhood has been in business since the 1930s. The 57-room Spanish-Colonial resort features arched entryways, covered ceilings, and ceramic floor tiles. Its location is within walking distance of both the Uptown Design District and shopping and dining downtown. Beautiful pool, restaurant and bar, and spa. *Info*: 572 N. Indian Canyon Dr. Tel. 760/969-1800. www.colonypalmshotel.com.

Los Arboles $$

The comfortable rooms of this quaint hotel have rich wood furnishings and mosaic tile bathrooms. The pool has a hot tub, and there's a bonus: the popular **El Mirasol Mexican Restaurant** is here, with a large outdoor dining patio. *Info*: 784 N Indian Canyon Dr. Tel. 760/459-3605. losarboleshotel.com.

Movie Colony $$-$$$

The Movie Colony was once frequented by stars like Dinah Shore, Cary Grant, and Jack Benny. Today, this hotel is a study of minimalist and modernist architecture. Designed by mid-century modern architect Albert Frey in the 1930s, this boutique hotel has private patios and a great location within walking distance of the Uptown Design District and downtown. Lovely pool! *Info*: 726 N. Indian Canyon Dr. Tel. 760/284-1600. moviecolonyhotel.com.

SLEEPING & EATING

Sleeping
1. Ace
2. Alcazar
3. ARRIVE
4. Avalon
5. Caliente Tropics
6. Casa Cody
7. Cole Hotel
8. Colony Palms
9. Del Marcos
10. Drift
11. Fleur Noire
12. Holiday House
13. Hotel California
14. Hotel Zoso
15. Ingleside Inn
16. Kimpton Rowan
17. La Serena Villas
18. Los Arboles
19. Margaritaville
20. Movie Colony
21. Orbit In
22. Palm Springs Hotel
23. Parker
24. Renaissance
25. Saguaro
26. Sparrows
27. Triada
28. V Hotel
29. Villa Royale
30. The Weekend

The Palm Springs Hotel $$-$$$
Desert-modernist architecture, modern amenities, and a relaxing vibe are at this hotel on the northern end of town. Nice pool and updated rooms (the hotel was renovated in the last few years). Some suites have a separate living area. Come here to relax in a small hotel a bit away from the downtown crowds. *Info*: 2135 N Palm Canyon Dr. Tel. 760/459-1255. www.thepalmspringshotel.com.

Margaritaville $$
The famous Riviera Hotel, once the haunt of the Rat Pack, has now been converted into a Margaritaville Resort. On the north end of town, it has a fabulous pool and several eateries. *Info*: 1600 N. Indian Canyon Dr. at Vista Chino. Tel. 760/327-8311. www.margaritavilleresorts.com.

Fleur Noire $$
Adults only at this boutique hotel with 21 casitas, bungalows, and suites. Bold floral wall murals are featured throughout the property. Rooms are equipped with refrigerators and most rooms also have a wet bar. There's a champagne and rose bar at the clubhouse. *Info*: 1555 N. Indiana Canyon Dr. Tel. 760/459-3865. fleurnoirehotel.com.

Triada $$-$$$
This Spanish-Colonial hotel is close to both the Uptown Design District and downtown. Upgraded rooms have kitchenettes. There's a restaurant on the premises serving Californian cuisine. Two pools, a hot tub, and a gym are some of the amenities. *Info*: 640 N. Indian Canyon Dr. Tel. 760/844-7000. www.triadapalmsprings.com.

The Weekend $$-$$$
Many of the homes of the stars featured in this book are within walking distance of the Old Las Palmas neighborhood. This small, mid-century modern boutique hotel has recently been renovated. Suites have a bedroom and a living area. Some have kitchenettes. Really, a lovely property with a pool and parking. The property is now adults only. *Info*: 111 S. Via Lola. Tel. 760/303-4162. www.theweekendpalmsprings.com.

SLEEPING & EATING 95

Central/Downtown
Avalon $$$
Luxury and interesting design at this attractive property. There are three pools (two of which are for adults only), a poolside restaurant (**ChiChi**), and a groovy cocktail lounge. *Info*: 415 S. Belardo Rd. Tel. 760/318-3012. www.avalon-hotel.com/palm-springs/.

Casa Cody $$
The oldest-operating hotel in Palm Springs was built in the 1920s. Southwestern decor, rooms of varying sizes, and two pools.. The property allows kids and pets. *Info*: 175 S. Cahuilla Rd. Tel. 760/320-9346. www.casacody.com.

Del Marcos Hotel $$$
Designed by William F. Cody in 1947, this 17-room modernist hotel is found in the Tennis Club neighborhood near downtown. Built of stone and redwood, the rooms were designed to surround the pool and show off the stunning mountain views. *Info*: 225 W. Baristo Rd. (at S. Belardo Rd.). Tel. 760/325-6902. www.delmarcoshotel.com. *Also see page 21.*

Holiday House $$$
A blue-and-white theme for this 1950s hotel. There are 28 rooms with a central pool, restaurant, loaner bikes, and a bar. Adults only at this mid-century modern classic. Location is perfect for walking downtown to restaurants and shops. There are no TVs in the rooms, but you shouldn't be watching television on vacation, anyway. Oh, and they have a great shuttle bus! (*pictured at right*) *Info*: 200 W. Arenas Rd. Tel. 760/320-8866. www.holidayhouseps.com.

Drift
Opened in 2023, this hotel has a large swimming pool with cabanas, free bikes, a restaurant, and a bar. It's conveniently located near all the action. Some rooms have kitchens. A good addition to downtown. *Info*: 284 S. Indian Canyon Dr. Tel. 888/976-4483. drifthotels.co/palmsprings.

Ingleside Inn $$-$$$
Built in the 1920s and recently renovated, this wonderful 30-room hotel has quite the history. Enjoy a martini by the pool, just like the Rat Pack did. **Melvyn's Restaurant** is here, with its lively piano bar. Adults only. *Info*: 200 W. Ramon Rd. Tel. 760/325-0046. www.inglesideinn.com.

Kimpton Rowan $$$
This 153-room hotel has opened in the new downtown-development area. At the rooftop pool and bar, you'll have some of the best views in the city. There are two restaurants here (*see page 106*), and plenty within walking distance. *Info*: 100 W. Tahquitz Canyon Way. Tel. 760/904-5015. www.rowanpalmsprings.com.

La Serena Villas $$$
Although it was built in the 1930s, this beautiful and serene 18-room boutique hotel was renovated in 2016. There's a popular on-site restaurant (**Azúcar**), a spa, and a fabulous rooftop bar to watch the sunset. *Info*: 339 S. Belardo Rd. Tel. 844/932-8044. laserenavillas.com.

Orbit In $$-$$$
This funky and fun inn is where to stay to experience mid-century style. All rooms face the pool, and most have kitchenettes. Use one of the cruiser bikes to take in the downtown area. Join other guests for an "Orbitini" around the pool. *Info*: 562 W. Arenas Rd. Tel. 760/323-3585. www.orbitin.com.

Renaissance $$
This large hotel is located between the airport and downtown, and it's just a short walk to the convention center. The outdoor pool has private cabanas, and there's an on-site restaurant and lounge. There's also a children's pool. Schedule a massage or workout in the gym. *Info*: 888 Tahquitz Canyon Way. Tel. 760/322-6000. www.marriot.com.

Hotel Zoso $$
You can't beat the location of this centrally located, 163-room hotel in downtown Palm Springs. You're near restaurants, LGBTQ+ nightlife on Arenas Road, and just three blocks from the convention center. Large pool and lively cocktail lounge. *Info*: 150 S. Indian Canyon Dr. Tel. 760/325-9676. www.hotelzosopalmsprings.com.

SLEEPING & EATING

South
Ace Hotel & Swim Club $$-$$$
What used to be a chain hotel with a Denny's restaurant is now a hipster hotel. The attraction here is the large pool with frequent pool parties, and poolside drink and food service. Get rid of your stress at The Feel Good Spa, enjoy a classic cocktail at the Amigo Room, then dinner at **The Kings Highway Diner**. *Info*: 701 E. Palm Canyon Dr., Tel. 760/325-9900. www.acehotel.com/palmsprings.

Caliente Tropics $$-$$$
Walk through the A-frame entrance of this "Polynesian" hotel, grab a tropical drink at the bar, follow the tiki torches to the large pool, have a bite at the restaurant, and you'll "dig" why this was a Rat Pack hangout. *Info*: 411 E. Palm Canyon Rd. Tel. 760/327-1391. www.calientetropics.com.

Hotel California $$
Welcome to the Hotel California—where you can chill at the pool, borrow a bike to tour the city, or prepare a meal at the communal grill. Built in the 1940s in the Spanish-Mission style, rooms have been updated but have kept their rustic charm. *Info*: 424 E. Palm Canyon Dr. Tel. 760/322-8855. www.palmspringshotelcalifornia.com.

Parker $$$
This luxury resort has tennis courts, two pools, upscale bar/restaurants, and a wine bar featuring the best of California wineries. Truly a pampered experience. Many exclusive events are held here, including some during the International Film Festival. *Info*: 4200 E. Palm Canyon Dr. Tel. 760/770-5000. www.theparkerpalmsprings.com.

Saguaro $$
Good location and plenty of events at this 244-room colorful hotel. With dining options, a large pool, two hot tubs, and an outdoor bar. It's a fun vibe, just perfect for a weekend getaway. The **El Jefe Restaurant** is also here. *Info*: 1800 E. Palm Canyon Dr. Tel. 760/323-1711. thesaguaro.com.

Sparrows $$-$$$

Hollywood stars hung out here in the 1950s, when it was the Red Barn. After a complete renovation, the rustic Sparrows now offers 20 garden and poolside rooms, each with its own patio. Great bar, and the **Barn Kitchen** serves innovative cuisine. You'll know you're there when you see the sign with two sparrows. Interesting, hip, and comfortable. *Info*: 1330 E. Palm Canyon Dr. Tel. 760/327-2300. sparrowslodge.com.

V Hotel $$-$$$

You'd never know this was a budget motel not too long ago. Now renovated, rooms and suites are available (many with balconies and patios). Two pools, a hot tub, pool bar, and a firepit and grill area are just some of the amenities. **Gigi's** restaurant serves desert-inspired, farm-to-table fare. *Info*: 333 E. Palm Canyon Dr. Tel. 617/300-0956. www.sonder.com.

Villa Royale $$$

Step back in time to old Hollywood. This 38-room resort, built in the 1940s, features three pools, a cozy bar, and the delicious **Del Rey** restaurant. The lush grounds are simply lovely. *Info*: 1620 S. Indian Trail. Tel. 760/327-2314. villaroyale.com.

Other Desert Cities
Agua Caliente Casino Resort $$-$$$

This modern casino/hotel complex off I-10, ten miles (16 km) outside Palm Springs in Rancho Mirage, has lots of dining options, and a theater for live concerts and performances. *Info*: 32-250 Bob Hope Dr., Rancho Mirage. Tel. 888/999-1995. www.aguacalientecasinos.com.

Hotel Paseo $$$

El Paseo, the "Rodeo Drive of the Desert," is known for its high-end boutiques, galleries, and restaurants. This hotel offers both rooms and suites, a pool, poolside bar, fitness center, spa, restaurant—or stay in their classic 1950s Airstream trailer. And then how about a little luxury shopping? *Info*: 45-400 Larkspur Lane, Palm Desert. Tel 760/340-9001. hotelpaseo.com.

SLEEPING & EATING

JW Marriott Desert Springs Resort $$-$$$
Two championship golf courses, five pools, tennis courts, fitness center, spa, several restaurants: you name it. You can even take a gondola tour of the waterways around the hotel. *Info*: 74-855 Country Club Dr., Palm Desert. Tel. 760/341-2211. www.marriott.com.

La Quinta Resort $$-$$$
The Coachella Valley is known for its huge resorts and spas. This complex has five golf courses, 41 (yes, 41) pools, spa, fitness centers, tennis courts, restaurants, and bars. This is where you go if you have no intention of leaving the property. *Info*: 49-499 Eisenhower Dr., La Quinta. Tel. 760/564-4111. laquintaresort.com.

Omni Rancho Las Palmas Resort $$-$$$
This large resort with 444 guest rooms has everything from a golf course to swimming pools to a business center (if you're inclined to do that to yourself on vacation). *Info*: 41-000 Bob Hope Dr., Rancho Mirage. Tel. 760/568-2727. www.omnihotels.com.

Sands Hotel and Spa $$$
Most hotels outside of Palm Springs and in the "other desert cities" tend to be huge and impersonal. The Sands offers 46 guest rooms, including two suites and one presidential suite, along with a spa and inviting pool. A popular destination for those who attend the nearby Indian Wells Tennis Garden events. *Info*: 44-985 Province Way, Indian Wells. Tel. 760/321-3771. sandshotelandspa.com.

LGBTQ+ RESORTS

North of Downtown
Trixie Motel: 210 W. Stevens Rd., Tel. 760/808-0014. Opened in 2022, the Trixie Motel is named after owner and drag queen Trixie Mattel. You can't miss this pink motel in the Old Las Palmas neighborhood. The renovation of the property was the subject of a Discovery television series. trixiemotel.com.

Canyon Club: 960 N. Palm Canyon Dr., Tel. 760/778-8042. Men's resort in the Uptown Design District. Rooms are centered around the pool and there's a large, frisky outdoor area.

Warm Sands
All Worlds Resort: 535 S. Warm Sands Dr., Tel. 760/323-7505. Clothing-optional resort with pool, hot tubs, and popular Maze play area. www.allworlds.com.
Desert Paradise: 615 S. Warm Sands Dr., Tel. 760/320-5650. Small clothing-optional resort with 12 rooms, pool, and hot tub. desertparadise.com.
Hacienda: 586 Warm Sands Dr., Tel. 760/327-8111. Clothing-optional resort with pool and nine suites. www.thehacienda.com.
El Mirasol Villas: 525 Warm Sands Dr., Tel. 760/327-5913. Clothing-optional resort with two pools (located in the former home of Howard Hughes). www.elmirasol.com.
INNdulge: 601 S. Grenfall Rd., Tel. 760/327-1408. Clothing-optional resort with pool and 12-person hot tub. inndulge.com.
Vista Grande: 574 S. Warm Sands Dr., Tel. 760/322-2404. Clothing-optional resort with three pools, 16-person hot tub, and waterfall. www.vistagranderesort.com.

South of Downtown
Santiago: 650 E. San Lorenzo Rd., Tel. 760/322-1300. Clothing-optional resort with pool and lounge. www.santiagoresort.com.
Triangle Inn: 555 E. San Lorenzo Rd., Tel. 760/322-7993. Clothing-optional resort with pool, hot tub, and lush gardens (and some lush guests, too). www.triangle-inn.com.

Cathedral City
CCBC: 68300 Gay Resort Dr., Tel. 760/324-1350. Clothing-optional resort with large pool, play areas, and adjoining restaurant (Runway). www.ccbcresorthotel.com.

SLEEPING & EATING

EATING
Dining in Palm Springs and the Coachella Valley tends to be a casual affair. There are, however, some high-end restaurants, where you'll find everything from authentic Mexican food to award-winning French cuisine. **Also see the *Sleeping* section for more recommendations.**

North/Uptown/Movie Colony
Paul Bar $$
Don't be put off by the strip mall location of this eatery. Step inside and you'll find a fun and fabulous bar serving delicious cocktails and tasty food. Options include steak frites, pan roasted salmon, and vegan yellow curry. One of our favorites! *Info*: 3700 E. Vista Chino. Tel. 760/656-4082. Open Wed-Sun at 4pm. Closed Mon and Tue. www.thepaulbarps.com.

Boozehounds $$
Bring your dogs to the outdoor patio at this contemporary space on the north end. There's a large restaurant, bar, and a coffee shop. Salads, burgers, and even fried smelt on the menu. Fun happy hour! *Info*: 2080 N Palm Canyon Dr. Tel. 760/656-0067. Open daily at 2pm (Fri-Sun at 10am) Closed Tue and Wed in summer. boozehoundsps.com.

Billy Reed's $-$$
A dedicated following at this restaurant on the north end. Billy Reed's has been around forever and you might wonder if your mother or grandmother decorated the dining areas while you peruse the huge menu. The desserts, created by the owner, are incredible. Good value, sizeable portions, lots of choices, and a comfortable way to dine in Palm Springs. *Info*: 1800 N. Palm Canyon Dr. Tel. 760/325-1946. Open daily 8am-9pm. billyreedsps.com.

1501 Gastropub $$
This addition to the north end offers a range of seasonal food and a comprehensive drink selection. Everything from fish and chips to large salads like spicy sauteed shrimp Thai style. Attractive and airy location. Good weekend brunch and good service. *Info*: 1501 N. Palm Canyon Dr. Tel. 760/320-1501. Open daily for lunch and dinner. 1501uptown.com.

Cheeky's $-$$ and Birba $$
Popular Cheeky's has an pleasant patio where you can enjoy brunch. Definitely try the BLT with jalapeño bacon, and down it with a delicious Bloody Mary. Expect to wait for a table! *Info*: 622 N. Palm Canyon Dr. Tel. 760/327-7595. Open Thu-Mon 8am-2pm. Closed Tue, Wed, and part of summer. www.cheekysps.com. Next door is **Birba $$**. Owned by the

Dining Prices

Prices for a main course:
- $$$$ Very Expensive: over $30 • $$$ Expensive: $21-$30
- $$ Moderate: $10-$20 • $ Inexpensive: under $10

Eating
1. Bill's Pizza
   Farm
   French Miso Cafe
   Grand Central
   Tyler's
2. Billy Reed's
   Boozehounds
3. Birba
   Cheeky's
   Jake's
4. Bongo Johnny's
5. Chef Tanya's Kitchen
6. Copley's
7. Elmer's
8. El Mirasol
9. Eight4Nine
10. Felipe's
11. Fisherman's Market
    Shanghai Red's
    Il Giardino
12. 533 Viet Fusion
    Guiseppe's
13. Il Corso
    Juniper Table
    On The Mark
14. Johannes
    Thai Smile
15. John Henry's Cafe
16. Koffi
17. Le Vallauris
18. LULU
19. Miro's
    Bar Cecil
20. Mr. Lyon's
21. Paul Bar
22. Peppers Thai
23. Pinocchio in the Desert
24. Rick's Desert Grill
25. Rooster and the Pig
26. Sandwich Spot
27. Sandfish
28. Sherman's
29. Spencer's
30. Tac/Quila
31. Trio
32. V Wine Lounge
33. Workshop Kitchen
34. 1501 Uptown Gastropub

SLEEPING & EATING 103

same group, this lively Italian restaurant has a large patio, and serves good pasta dishes and pizza. *Info*: 622 N. Palm Canyon Dr. Tel. 760/327-5678. Open Wed-Sun 6pm-10pm. Closed Mon and Tue. www.iheartbirba.com.

Copley's $$$-$$$$
There's a large patio and lovely indoor dining at Cary Grant's former guesthouse. This is California dining at its best. Whether you have steak, lamb, fish, or duck, make sure you end your meal with the specialty basil ice cream. Expensive, but worth the cost for a unique Palm Springs experience. Open Tue-Sun for dinner. *Info*: 621 N. Palm Canyon Dr. Tel. 760/327-9555. Open at 5:30pm. Closed Mon and Tue. www.copleyspalmsprings.com.

Eight4Nine (849) $$-$$$
The city's former post office is now a fantastic restaurant with colorful contemporary decor. California cuisine, from sea bass to steaks. Lovely outdoor patio adds to the charm. Enjoyable brunch spot. *Info*: 849 N. Palm Canyon Dr. Tel. 760/325-8490. Open daily. www.eight4nine.com. The same group owns **Willie's**, serving modern fare in its attractive restaurant in Rancho Mirage. *Info*: 69830 Highway 111, Rancho Mirage. Tel. 760/202-4499. Open Tue-Sat at 5pm, Sun at 11am. www.williesrm.com.

El Mirasol $$
This festive restaurant serves classic Mexican food and delicious margaritas on the patio at Los Arboles Hotel, and there's a second location on the south end of town at 140 E. Palm Canyon Dr. *Info*: 266 E. Altamira with entry off N. Indian Canyon Dr. Tel. 760/459-3136. Closed Mon and Tue. elmirasolrest.com.

Jake's $$
This small restaurant, serving California cuisine, has both indoor and outdoor dining. Very good brunch and delicious desserts. A bonus is the small outdoor bar serving excellent cocktails and a spicy Bloody Mary. *Info*: 664 N. Palm Canyon Dr. Tel. 760/327-4400. Closed Mon-Wed and part of summer. www.jakespalmsprings.com.

Rick's Desert Grill $-$$
Casual and friendly with good Cuban cuisine at great prices and enormous glasses of wine. Try the delicious Cuban sandwich (and the fried chicken dinner when available). *Info*: 1596 N. Palm Canyon Dr. Tel. 760/325-2127. Open Mon-Sat at 4pm. Closed Sun. www.ricksdesertgrill.com. **Rick's** has another location at 1973 N. Palm Canyon Dr. serving delicious breakfasts and lunches. ricksrestaurant.biz.

Sandfish $$$
Japanese sushi and seafood at this trendy and starkly decorated restaurant across the street from the ARRIVE Hotel. Popular, so make reservations. Known for its list of rare whiskies. *Info*: 1556 N. Palm Canyon Rd. Tel 760/537-1022. Open daily for dinner. www.sandfishsushiwhiskey.com.

Trio $$-$$$
This popular, fun, and friendly restaurant with contemporary white-and-orange decor, California cuisine, and a great bar scene is a favorite with tourists and locals. Great afternoon menu, and fantastic martini specials. *Info*: 707 N. Palm Canyon Dr.
Tel. 760/864-8746. Open Wed-Mon at 4pm. Closed Tue. www.triopalmsprings.com.

Workshop Kitchen $$$-$$$$
Industrial-inspired space (concrete booths, communal tables, and high ceilings) with innovative California fare and excellent cocktails. Large following from Los Angeles. *Info*: 800 N. Palm Canyon Dr. Tel. 760/459-3451. Open daily for dinner. www.workshopkitchenbar.com.

Central/Downtown
Bill's Pizza $-$$
Located in the historic La Plaza area in the middle of downtown, this popular pizza place serves pies with a sourdough crust. Toppings include sausage from Italy, caramelized onions, fresh basil, and sheep's-milk feta. Gluten-free pizza is also available. Wash it all down with a beer or decent house red wine. *Info*: 119 S. Indian Canyon Dr. Tel. 760/325-5771. Open daily at 11am. www.billspizzapalmsprings.com. There's a second location in Palm Desert at 73196 California Highway 111. Tel. 760/834-8476.

Bongo Johnny's $$
This gay-owned restaurant is on the second floor at the corner of N. Palm Canyon Dr. and W. Amado Rd. Much of the restaurant is open air, so you'll have good views of the city's main street. There's a relaxed vibe here, and the food will not disappoint. Burgers, sandwiches, salads, and a popular brunch. *Info*: 301 N. Palm Canyon Dr. Tel. 760/318-3960. Open daily 8am-8pm (Fri and Sat until 9pm). www.bongojohnnys.com.

Fisherman's Market/Shanghai Red's $$

Our friends from the UK said that the fish and chips here were just as good as there. Order at the counter, and the food is then brought to your table (many of which are outside). The fish fry is great, but if you want fish grilled or blackened, they'll do that too. If ordering at the counter isn't your thing, you can dine at **Shanghai Red's** inside (Wed-Sun), where you'll find excellent fish tacos. They often have live music. *Info*: 235 South Indian Canyon Dr. Tel. 760/327-1766. Open daily 11am-9pm. www.fishermans.com.

French Miso Cafe $$

This totally cute restaurant is in a small courtyard off La Plaza in downtown Palm Springs. The food is French with Japanese influences. Try the pork ginger (pork braised with onions and mushrooms in a soy/ginger broth) or the chicken paillard. Down it all with a glass of French wine, champagne, or sake. *Info*: 19 La Plaza. Tel. 760/699-7730. Closed Mon and Tue. www.frenchmisocafe.com.

Grand Central $$

Located downtown at La Plaza, this restaurant (in a former department store) is a perfect stop while shopping or strolling downtown. Delicious brunch, and seasonal California cuisine. Try the flat-iron steak salad or the watermelon gazpacho. Good cocktails at the large bar. *Info*: 160 La Plaza. Tel. 760/699-7185. Open daily. No dinner on Sun and Mon. 7:30am-3pm. www.grandcentralpalmsprings.com.

Il Corso $$$

Authentic Italian dishes—including homemade pastas, wood-oven pizza, and seafood—with an emphasis on Sicilian dishes, as the chef is from the island. Good wine list. *Info*: 111 N Palm Canyon Dr., Suite 180. Tel. 760/656-3700. Open daily at 4pm. springs.ilcorsodining.com. There's a location in Palm Desert at 73520 El Paseo Suite B. Tel. 760/341-6700. Closed Sun.

Il Giardino $$-$$$

Our favorite Italian restaurant in the city. Try the *capellini puttanesca* (angel-hair pasta with tomato sauce, olives, capers, and garlic) or the flavorful *vitello piccata al limone* (veal scaloppine with lemon, capers, and vegetables). Interesting Italian wine list. *Info*: 333 S. Indian Canyon Dr. Tel. 760/322-0888. Closed Sun. ilgiardinopalmsprings.com.

Johannes $$$
It's hot in the desert, so *wiener schnitzel* isn't the first thing that comes to mind when you're dining out. The menu here is eclectic Austrian and Asian fare (there's a mix) with a diverse wine list. Great downtown location. *Info*: 196 S. Indian Canyon Dr. (at Arenas Rd.). Tel. 760/778-0017. Closed Mon and Tue. www.johannespalmsprings.com.

Juniper Table $$
This restaurant, on the first floor of the Kimpton Rowan Hotel downtown, features hot and cold breakfast items, sandwiches, salads, and shareable plates. Among dinner choices are *steak frites* and the delicious JT Burger, made with either Black Angus beef or Impossible meat. *Info*: 100 W Tahquitz Canyon Way. Tel. 760/904-5032. Open daily for breakfast, brunch and dinner. www.junipertable.com. For more upscale dining, head to the rooftop restaurant **4 Saints** ($$$). www.4saintspalmsprings.com

Le Vallauris $$$-$$$$
Nestled against the mountains in downtown near the art museum, this French restaurant is a romantic destination. Attentive service and traditional French cuisine, such as beef filet with a cabernet reduction. *Info*: 385 W. Tahquitz Canyon Way. Tel. 760/325-5059. Open daily for dinner. Sunday brunch. Closed in summer. www.levallauris.com.

On The Mark $-$$
Located in the heart of downtown, this gourmet food market and deli is the perfect place to visit if you're looking to stock up for your hotel room or rental. You'll find artisan cheese, snacks, craft beer, and wine. *Info*: 111 N. Palm Canyon Dr. Tel. 760/832-8892. Open daily 10am-5pm. onthemarkpalmsprings.com.

Peppers Thai/Thai Smile $$
These two will fill all your Thai food needs. Peppers Thai has little ambiance, but delicious food. Try the yellow curry with potato, onion, and carrots. Thai Smile has a great location, and fun vibe. Try the panang curry. *Info*: Peppers: 396 N Palm Canyon Dr, Tel. 760/322-1259. Closed Mon. www.peppersthai.com. Thai Smile: 100 S. Indian Canyon Dr. Tel. 760/320-5503. Open daily. www.thaismileps.com.

SLEEPING & EATING 107

LULU $$-$$$
This California bistro is on the busiest intersection in downtown. Although the food isn't always fantastic, the scene is. Friendly service and generous portions from the large menu serving California/American cuisine. Freshly baked bread and sinful desserts are made in-house daily. The large bar has perhaps the desert's longest happy hour. You can sit inside or outside on the large terrace, where the people-watching is great. *Info*: 200 S. Palm Canyon Dr. Tel. 760/327-5858. Open daily. www.lulupalmsprings.com.

Pinocchio in the Desert $-$$
Casual outdoor dining downtown. Not just your usual breakfast and lunch items, but also Hawaiian pancakes, Mexican schnitzel, and lobster benedict. Admit it, you really came for the bottomless champagne for $7.95 per person. Also open for dinner. *Info*: 134 E Tahquitz Canyon Way. Tel. 760/322-3776. Open daily. pinocchiops.com.

Pomme Frite $$-$$$
Belgian and French specialties, with indoor and patio dining, and known for its steamed black mussels. Try the *steak frites* (steak and french fries), or the delicious *coq au vin* (chicken braised in red wine with bacon, onions, mushrooms, and herbs). Extensive selection of Belgian beer. *Info*: 256 S Palm Canyon Dr. Tel. 760/778-3727. Closed Tue and Wed. pomme-frite.com.

Rooster and the Pig $$
One of our favorites, this industrial-chic restaurant does not take reservations, but even if you have to wait for a table, it's worth it. The innovative Vietnamese fare is unlike anything else in the city. The panko-crusted chicken-stuffed curry ball and the lemongrass pork skewers are worth the trip. Highly recommended. *Info*: 356 S. Indian Canyon Dr. Tel. 760/832-6691. Open Wed-Sun 5pm-9pm. Closed Mon and Tue and part of Aug. www.roosterandthepig.com.

Sandwich Spot $
You don't have to spend a lot of money for good food. This eatery is in an arcade off the main street. Great sandwiches like the MILF (chicken, cheese, and cranberry) and Philly steak. Nice outdoor patio for dining. *Info*: 276 N. Palm Canyon Dr. Tel. 760/778-7900. Open daily 11am-6pm. thesandwichspot.com.

Sherman's $-$$
Always jammed, this restaurant and bakery downtown serves deli favorites such as corned beef on rye with potato salad or coleslaw. A Palm Springs institution since 1963. *Info*: 401 E Tahquitz Canyon Way. Tel. 760/325-1199. Open daily 8am-9pm. www.shermansdeli.com. Also in Palm Desert at 73-161 Country Club Dr. Tel. 760/568-1350.

Spencer's $$$
This lovely spot is tucked away in the Palm Springs Tennis Club and is a favorite of locals and visitors alike. Lovely patio and delicious food. A specialty here is the Maine lobster club with mayo, bacon, lettuce, tomato, and avocado. Great place to spend a special lunch or dinner. *Info*: 701 W. Baristo Rd. Tel. 760/327-3446. Closed Tue and Wed .www.spencersrestaurant.com.

Tac/Quila $$
Modern Mexican cuisine in an attractive setting at this downtown eatery. Try the excellent *carne asada* street tacos with guacamole and *pico de gallo* in a corn tortilla. Known for their interesting cocktails. *Info*: 415 N. Palm Canyon Dr. Tel. 760/417-4471. Open daily. tacquila.com. **Clandestino** ($$), by the same owners, also features modern Mexican cuisine in its downtown location overlooking the art museum. 175 N. Palm Canyon Dr. Tel 760/699-6222. Open daily at noon.

Farm $$$
This fantastic restaurant located just off La Plaza in a lovely setting serves innovative dishes from the south of France. *Info*: 6 La Plaza. Tel. 760/322-2724. Breakfast and lunch daily. Dinner Fri-Tue. www.farmpalmsprings.com.

Tyler's $-$$
You may have to wait a while to get into this popular eatery located downtown in La Plaza, but it's worth it: The burgers are excellent! Other choices include a delicious veggie burger, chicken salad, and BLTA (bacon, lettuce, tomato, and avocado). Add beer or wine and one (or two) of their delicious side dishes, and you have the perfect lunch. *Info*: 149 S. Indian Canyon Dr. Tel. 760/325-2990. Open Mon-Sat 11am-4pm. Closed Sun and part of summer. www.tylersburgers.com.

SLEEPING & EATING 109

V Wine Lounge $$
Without a doubt, the best place to sample wine. This friendly and chill wine bar is known for serving lesser-known varietals. The *charcuterie* and cheese boards add to the experience. A large horseshoe-shaped bar and ample outdoor patio add to the atmosphere. *Info*: 600 E. Tahquitz Canyon Way. Tel. 760/668-9665. Open daily at 3pm. vwinelounge.com.

South
Bar Cecil $$$-$$$$
Contemporary bistro fare is served in a dining room decorated with original art (including Andy Warhol's *After the Party*). There's an attractive wood and marble bar with tufted turquoise stools. Entrees include ratatouille, smoked bone-in pork chop, *steak frites*, and pan-seared halibut. Thirsty? Try the Beluga Gold Vodka martini for $50! *Info*: 1555 S. Palm Canyon Dr. Tel. 442/332-3800. Open Tue-Sun at 5pm. barcecil.com.

Chef Tanya's Kitchen $-$$
Don't let the neighborhood distract you. This vegan lunch counter, deli, and grocery is worth the trip. Try the Cubano (slow-roasted citrus and garlic seitan), Chupacabra (sliced crispy seitan filets, avocado, cilantro, and house-pickled jalapeños), or the CTK Burger (made with tempeh on a potato bun). *Info*: 706 S. Eugene Rd. Tel. 760/832-9007. Open daily 11am-8pm. Also at 72695 Highway 111 in Palm Desert. Tel. 760/636-0863. Open daily 9am-9pm. www.cheftanyaskitchen.com.

Elmer's $-$$
Breakfast, lunch, and dinner at this popular diner. Large menu. If you're there for breakfast, make sure you try the classic German pancake with lemon wedges, whipped butter, and powdered sugar. Filling! *Info*: 1030 E. Palm Canyon Dr. Tel. 760/327-8419. Open daily 6am-9pm. eatatelmers.com.

Felipe's $-$$
Authentic Mexican cuisine at this family-owned restaurant with a large outdoor patio, in a strip mall near the airport. Known for their fresh seafood dishes and excellent margaritas. Try the *torta cubana*, a pulled pork sandwich. Friendly service. *Info*: 400 S. El Cielo Rd. #8. Tel. 760/318-9274. Open daily 9am-9pm. They also have an interest in the Mexican restaurant **El Patio** downtown at 139 E. Andreas Rd. Tel. 760/832-6332. Open daily. elpatiopalmsprings.com.

533 Viet Fusion $$-$$$
Pho, vermicelli, pad thai, wok-fried rice, and vegetarian dishes are just some choices at this upscale Vietnamese restaurant. Try the red-curry coconut-broth tiger shrimp, or the chicken-lemongrass meatballs. Wine and beer are also served. *Info*: 1775 E. Palm Canyon Dr., Suite 625. Tel. 760/778-6595. Closed Mon. www.533vietfusion.com.

Guiseppe's $$
Chicago-style pizza and pasta dishes (try the portabella mushroom ravioli) at this popular and cozy Italian restaurant. *Info*: 1775 E Palm Canyon Dr. Tel. 760/537-1890. Open daily at 4pm. giuseppesps.com.

John Henry's Cafe $$
Classic American cuisine served in an enchanting courtyard with twinkling lights, table candles, and wonderful service. A popular spot—in a somewhat obscure location. *Info*: 1785 E. Tahquitz Canyon Way. Tel. 760/327-7667. Closed Mon and part of summer. johnhenryscafe.com.

Koffi $
The local favorite, for coffee, with four locations: 515 N. Palm Canyon Dr., 650 E Tahquitz Canyon Way, 1700 South Camino Real, and 71-380 Highway 111 in Rancho Mirage. Tel. 760/416-2244 (Palm Springs location). Open daily. kofficoffee.com.

Miro's $$-$$$
When you think of dining in the desert, beef Stroganoff or osso buco probably aren't top of mind. You'll find both Mediterranean and Central-European dishes here. An extensive and interesting wine list completes the experience. *Info*: 1555 S. Palm Canyon Dr. (in the Plaza del Sol Shopping Center). Tel. 760/323-5199. Open Tue-Sun at 5pm. Closed Mon www.mirospalmsprings.com.

Mr. Lyon's $$$
Your destination for beef: excellent prime rib, bone-in ribeye, filet mignon, and New York strip. They also serve fish and chicken. Known for their classic cocktails. *Info*: 233 E. Palm Canyon Dr. Tel. 760/327-1551. Open Wed-Sun at 5pm. Closed Mon and Tue. www.mrlyonsps.com.

6. Shopping

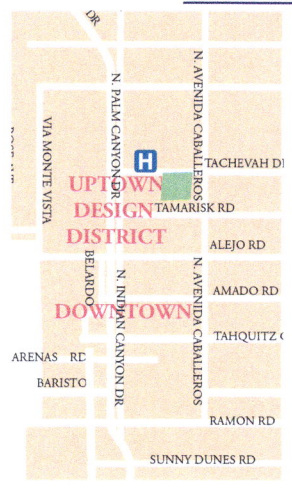

The **Uptown Design District** is north of Alejo Road. You'll find plenty of stores along N. Palm Canyon Drive, with lots of shops featuring mid-century modern furniture and accessories. **Downtown** is south of Alejo Road, where you'll find some touristy shops. Larger retailers (H&M, Sephora, and West Elm) are found around the Kimpton Rowan Hotel. Here are some of our favorite shopping destinations.

Uptown Design District
Just Fabulous
Books, gifts, cards, candles, art, household items, and celebrity book signings: like they say, just fabulous (and fun!). *Info*: 515 N. Palm Canyon Dr. Tel. 760/864-1300. Open daily. www.bjustfabulous.com.

The Frippery
Vintage clothing and accessories for the desert (and Hi-Desert) lifestyle. *Info*: 664 N. Palm Canyon Dr. Tel. 760/699-5365. Open Fri and Sat 11am-5pm, Sun and Mon 11am-4pm. Closed Tue-Thu. www.thefrippery.com.

Shag
Colorful, retro original art, prints, and home accessories by Josh Agle. *Info*: 725 N. Palm Canyon Dr. Tel. 760/322-3400. Open daily 10am-5pm (Fri-Sun until 8pm). www.shagstore.com.

Christopher Anthony
Vintage furnishings, art, sculpture, and lighting, with an emphasis on mid-century modern. Take your time and browse. *Info*: 803 N. Palm Canyon Dr. Tel. 760/322-0600. Open daily Mon, Wed-Sat 10am-5pm, Sun noon-5pm. Closed Tue. www.christopheranthonyltd.com.

Posh Pet Care
Just because you're on vacation doesn't mean you should forget your favorite fur person. This little shop has plenty of fun stuff for your pet and if you brought them along, they also offer grooming. *Info*: 844 N. Palm Canyon Dr. Tel. 760/318-7674. Open daily 9am-6pm. app.poshpetcare.com.

Michael Weems Collection
Elegant glassware, irreverent coasters, fun art, and interesting jewelry at this fun and quirky shop. *Info*: 384 N. Palm Canyon Dr. Tel. 760/534-1805. Closed Tue and Wed. www.michaelweems.com.

A La MOD
Vintage high-end mid-century modern furnishings and accessories (fabulous lamps). *Info*: 866 N. Palm Canyon Dr. Tel. 760/327-0707. Closed Tue. www.alamodps.com.

Trina Turk
Funky, fashionable clothing for women and men (and a household-goods section) housed in a 1960s mid-century modern building. *Info*: 891 N. Palm Canyon Dr. Tel. 760/416-2856. Open Mon-Thu 10am-6pm, Fri and Sat 10am-7pm, Sun 11am-5pm. www.trinaturk.com.

The Shops at Thirteen Forty-Five
Step inside this 1950s mid-century modern building and you'll find 13 shops selling interesting home accessories, art, clothing, jewelry, and furniture. *Info*: 1345 N. Palm Canyon Dr. Tel. 760/464-0480. Open Thu-Mon 11am-5pm. Closed Tue and Wed. www.theshopsat1345.com.

Re[X]
The largest design co-op in the city specializes in mid-century and modern furnishings and décor. *Info*: 2500 N. Palm Canyon Dr., Suite B1. Tel 760/656-0543. Open daily 11am-5pm. www.rex.haus.

Flannery Exchange
This mixed-use space combines office space and conference rooms with leisure activities. Boutiques include **Covet PS** (handcrafted jewelry), **Bobo PS** (stationery), and **Savage Art Gallery**. You can eat and drink at **Hoja Blanca** restaurant and **Café La Jefa**. *Info*: 750 N. Palm Canyon Dr. Tel. 760/364-9611. Open daily. www.flanneryexchange.com.

Downtown
Destination PSP
High-end Palm Springs souvenirs (housewares, swimwear, books, and more) at this shop. *Info*: 170 N. Palm Canyon Dr. Tel. 760/354-9154. Open daily 10am-6pm (Thu-Sat until 8pm). www.destinationpsp.com.

Sazzy's
Crafts, jewelry, pottery, and art from over 40 local and Southwest U.S. artists at this new edition to downtown. *Info*: 270 N. Palm Canyon Dr. Tel. 760/832-8332. Open daily 11am-5pm (Thu until 9pm, Fri-Sun until 6pm). Facebook: Sazzy's Galleria.

SHOPPING 113

Peepa's
Our favorite store in downtown Palm Springs. Fun, groovy, and friendly. Clothing (kaftan anyone?), artwork, novelties, gifts, cards, and household items. Just what you were hoping to find! *Info*: 120 N. Palm Canyon Dr. Tel. 760/318-3553. Open Mon-Sat 10am-9pm, Sun 11am-7pm. www.peepasps.com.

Palm Springs General Store
There are many souvenir shops in downtown Palm Springs, including this one filled with trinkets, gifts, and a large selection of T-shirts. *Info*: 193 S. Palm Canyon Dr. Tel. 760/320-7613. Open daily. www.psgeneralstore.com.

Mojave Flea Trading Post
Fifty artisans, merchants, and designers from the Coachella Valley, Hi-Desert, and beyond offer a mix of goods inspired by the desert. Apparel, apothecary, home accessories, art, and flowers all at this "bohemian" department store. Specialty food, beer, and wine can be purchased at **Palm Springs Bottle Shop**. *Info*: 383 N Indian Canyon Dr. Tel. 760/232-6132. Open daily 11am-5pm. shoptradingpost.com.

Imageville
Gary Dorothy's photography is featured at this shop. Wonderful images of the city and the desert. *Info*: 128 La Plaza. Tel. 760/416-9825. Open noon-5pm. Closed Thu. www.imageville.us.

Stewart Galleries
You'll find an eclectic mix of international fine art, unique designer furnishings, and an impressive collection of Majolica pottery. *Info*: 191 S. Indian Canyon Dr. (at Arenas Rd.). Tel. 760/325-0878. Open daily 11am-4pm. www.stewartgalleries.com.

Thick as Thieves
Small shop offering apparel, jewelry, household goods, rugs, and more, with an ever-changing, interesting inventory. *Info*: 183 S. Indian Canyon Dr. Tel. 760/832-8350. Open daily 11am-4pm. www.shopthieves.com.

Other Desert Cities
El Paseo
This high-end shopping district, called the "Rodeo Drive of the Desert," has designer boutiques—from Ralph Lauren to Riga—art galleries, upscale restaurants...You get the picture. *Info*: El Paseo, Palm Desert. A 14-mile (22.5 km) drive from downtown Palm Springs. www.elpaseocatalogue.com.

7. PLANNING YOUR TRIP/PRACTICAL MATTERS

Arriving
Palm Springs International Airport (PSP) is one of the most beautiful airports in the U.S., and most of it is open air. All major U.S. and Canadian airlines service the airport. There are several restaurants, bars, and wine bars where you can relax while waiting for your flight to depart. There are also several small stores where you can pick up a last-minute souvenir. The airport is located within the city limits at 3400 East Tahquitz Canyon Way. Tel. 760/318-3800. www.palmspringsairport.com.

Many travelers fly into the following airports:
Ontario, CA (ONT): 72 miles/116 kilometers
Santa Ana (SNA): 100 miles/161 kilometers
Los Angeles (LAX): 110 miles /176 kilometers
San Diego (SAN): 146 miles/235 kilometers

Car Rental
All major car rental companies operate at PSP, located in the arrivals hall.

Taxis/Rideshare
If you want to take a taxi from the airport, go to the taxi line right outside baggage claim. Rideshare stands are also outside.

Practical Matters
Banking & Money
Call your credit card company or bank before you leave to tell them you'll be using your ATM or credit card outside your usual area. Many have automatic controls that can "freeze" your account if the computer program determines that there are charges outside your normal range.

ATMs (with fees, of course) are the easiest way to change money if you are visiting from outside the United States. You'll find them everywhere, including the airport.

Climate & Weather
We have sunny, clear blue skies 350 or more days a year. Rain is very rare. The summers can be brutal at times, although high humidity is uncommon. But, that's what all those pools are for!

PLANNING YOUR TRIP/PRACTICAL MATTERS 115

Average high temperature/low temperature °F and °C and days of rain:

High F	Low F	Month	High C	Low C	Rainfall (inches)
71	48	January	22	9	1.27
74	50	February	23	10	1.15
82	55	March	28	13	0.63
88	60	April	31	16	0.08
92	65	May	34	18	0.06
105	74	June	41	23	0.05
108	80	July	42	27	0.19
108	80	August	42	27	0.40
102	75	September	39	24	0.39
91	65	October	33	18	0.11
78	53	November	26	12	0.29
69	47	December	21	8	0.61

You should check www.weather.com before you leave.

Internet Access/Wi-Fi
Wi-Fi is available at most hotels, bars, cafes, and restaurants.

Packing/Dress
Never pack prescription drugs, eyeglasses, or valuables. Carry them on. Don't ruin your trip by having to lug around huge suitcases. Palm Springs is quite casual. It's okay to wear shorts and even flip-flops to dinner, except in more expensive restaurants.

Postal Services
The main post office is located at 333. N. Sunrise Way. If you need a stamp, many souvenir shops sell them with postcards.

Public Art
The city is dotted with public art projects. You'll see colorful bike stands, decorated benches, sculpture, and artwork throughout downtown and the Uptown Design District. Don't miss "Isabelle" by Julian Voss-Andreae near the Kimpton Rowan Hotel, who seems to disappear as you walk around her. *See photo on page 106.*

Public Parks and Pools
For a city of its size, Palm Springs has an excellent network of public facilities. If you're looking for a centrally located park, head to **Ruth Hardy Park** (700 Tamarisk Road), where you'll find a wellness area (with exercise stations),

eight public tennis courts, and 22 acres of park. The city's largest park (61 acres) is **Demuth Park** (4365 Mesquite Avenue) on the south side of town, with tennis and pickleball courts, baseball and soccer fields, and dog parks. The 38-acre **Sunrise Park,** at Sunrise Way between Ramon Road and E. Baristo Road, has basketball courts, a baseball field, and grills. Also here are the **Swim Center** (Tel. 760/323-8278) with an Olympic-size pool; and a **Skate Park** (Tel. 760/656-0024). Reserve through www.palmspringsca.gov.

Public Transportation
The SunLine Transit Agency runs a number of bus lines throughout the Coachella Valley (including Desert Hot Springs, Palm Springs, Indio, and Coachella). The cost of a ride is $1. For schedules visit www.sunline.org.

Restrooms
There aren't a lot of public restrooms. If you need to go, your best bet is to head (no pun intended) to the nearest bar or cafe. It's considered good manners to purchase something if you use the restroom.

Smoking
Smoking is prohibited in hotels, restaurants, bars, clubs, museums, and on public transportation. Smoking outdoors is also restricted in certain areas.

Tipping
Palm Springs is a tourist destination, and many workers rely on tips to make a living. Most people tip 20% at restaurants. If you are visiting from outside the United States, know that it is extremely rare for the tip to be included in your bill.

Tourist Information
The helpful tourist information center in Palm Springs is located at the Palm Springs Visitor Center. Free computer access. *Info*: 2901 North Palm Canyon Dr. Tel. 800/347-7746 or 760/778-8418. Open daily 10am-5pm. www.visitpalmsprings.com.

Web Sites
- Made Easy Travel Guides: www.madeeasytravelguides.com
- City of Palm Springs: www.palmspringsca.gov
- Palm Springs Tourism: www.visitpalmsprings.com
- U.S. State Department: www.state.gov

8. INDEX

Ace Hotel & Swim Club 35
Aerial Tramway 11
Agua Caliente Band of Cahuilla Indians 28
Agua Caliente Casinos 33
Agua Caliente Cultural Museum 28
air museum 16
airport 114
Albert Frey House II 15, 18
Alexander Steel Houses 18
Aluminaire House 13
American Documentary Film Fest 42
Annenberg 26
architecture 15, 18
Architectural Design Center 15
Arenas Road 30
ARRIVE Hotel (pool) 35
arriving 114
art museum 13
art, outsider 86

banking 114
Big Bear 90
biking 50, 54, 67 (Joshua Tree)
birdwatching 84
Bob Hope House 24

Cabazon 82-83
Cabazon Dinosaurs 82
Cabot's Pueblo Museum 58
cacti/succulents 25
camping (Joshua Tree) 67
car rental 114
casinos 32-33, 83
cemetery (Desert Memorial Park) 41
Christmas parade 54
Cinema Diverse 42
City Hall 20
City National Bank Building 20

climate 114-115
clothes 115
Coachella music festival 53
Coachella Valley Preserve 56-57
Coachella Valley Savings & Loan buildings 21
concerts 75
contemporary art 54
Cornelia White House 28
crystal cave 72

date farm 57
day trips 81-90
Del Marcos Hotel 21
Desert Hills Premium Outlets (Cabazon) 83
Desert Hot Springs 58-59
Desert X 54
Dinah, The 53
dining 101-110
dinosaurs 82
documentary film festival 42
dressing (clothes) 115

East Jesus 86
eating 101-110
El Morocco Inn & Spa 36
El Paseo (shopping) 113
Elrod House 22
Elvis Honeymoon Hideaway 29
events 53-56
excursions 81-90

Fantasy Springs Resort Casino 33
Faye Sarkowsky Sculpture Garden 13
Festival of Lights 54
festivals 53-56
film festivals 42
flea market 72
Forever Marilyn 27

Frey House II 15, 18
gardens 15, 25, 26
gay 30-31, 53, 100
gay film festival 42
Giant Rock 74
golfing 51-52, 54

Hi-Desert/High Desert 70-79
hiking 44-49, 56-57, 79-80
hiking (Idyllwild) 87
historical society 28
Hollywood 38-43
Homes of the Stars 38-41
horseback riding (Joshua Tree) 68
hotels (Palm Springs) 91-98,
   (other desert cities) 99-100
House of Tomorrow 29

Idyllwild 87-89
Impressionist art 26
Indian Canyons 47-48
Indian Wells Tennis Garden 53
Integratron 74
International Film Festival 42
Internet access 115

Joshua Tree National Park 61-70
Joshua Tree (town) 76-78

Kaufmann House 22
Kimpton Rowan Hotel (pool) 36
Kocher Samson Building 23

Landers 74-75
lesbian festival 53
LGBTQ+ 30-31, 42, 53, 100
LGBTQ+ film festival 42
LGBTQ+ resorts 100
Living Desert Zoo and Gardens 15

mall, shopping 83
McCallum Adobe 28
Mid-Century Modern 15, 18-25
modern art 54

Modernism 15, 18-25
Modernism Week 26, 54
money 114
Monkey Tree Hotel 23
Monroe, Marilyn (statue) 27
Moorten Botanical Garden and
   Cactarium 25
Morongo Casino Resort and
   Spa 32
Morongo Valley 70
mountains 11, 49, 87, 90
Mount Jacinto State Park 11, 49
Museum of Ancient Wonders
   (MoAW) 32
music festivals 53

Nixon, Richard 26

orchid farm/tour 74
outlets (shopping) 83
outsider art 86

packing 115
Palm Desert 13, 17, 113
Palm Desert Half Marathon 55
Palm Springs Aerial Tramway 11
Palm Springs Air Museum 15
Palm Springs Art Museum 13
Palm Springs Historical Society 28
Palm Springs International Film
   Festival 42
Palm Springs International
   ShortFest 42
Palm Springs Visitor Center 12
Palm Springs Welcome Sign 12
Pappy & Harriets 73
Paseo, El (shopping) 113
pickleball 52
Pioneertown 73
pools 35-36, 116
postal service 115
Post-Impressionist art 26
Presley, Elvis 29
Pride festival and parade 53

public art 115
public parks 115-116
public pools 116
public transportation 116
Pueblo Museum 58

Racquet Club Cottages West 23
rainfall 114-115
Rat Pack 43
rentals, vacation 91
restaurants 101-110
restrooms 116
rideshare 101-110
rock climbing (Joshua Tree) 68
Rowan (Kimpton) Hotel (pool) 36
Ruddy's General Store 29
running 54, 56

Saguaro Hotel (pool) 36
Salton Sea 83-86
Salvation Mountain 86
Sand to Snow National Monument 79-80
Santa Fe Savings & Loan building 15, 18
sculpture garden 13
Shields Date Farm 57
Ship of the Desert 24
shopping (Cabazon) 113
shopping (other desert cities) 83
shopping (Palm Springs) 111-113
short film festival 42
short term vacation rentals 91
skate park 116
skiing, snow 90
Slab City 86
sleeping (Palm Springs) 91-98, (other desert cities) 99-100
smoking 116
Sonny Bono Salton Sea National Wildlife Refuge 84
Spa Resort Casino 32
spas 32, 35, 36, 58-59
Splash House 36, 56

Spotlight 29 Casino 32
Stagecoach music festival 53
stars homes 38-41
State Park 11
steel houses 18
street festival 55
St. Theresa Catholic Church 24
Sunnylands 26
swimming 35-36, 116

taxi 114
temperatures 114-115
tennis 52, 53
tipping 116
Tortoise Rock Casino 32
tourist information 12, 18, 116
Tram Road Challenge 56
Tramway 11
Tramway Gas Station 18
Trixie Motel 100
Tour de Palm Springs 54
Twentynine Palms 78-79

UFO 74-75

vacation rentals 91
Village Fest 55
Village Green Heritage Center 28-29
Visitor Center (Palm Springs) 12, 18, 116

Walk of the Inns 55
Walk of the Stars 42
weather 114-115
websites 116
Welcome Sign (Palm Springs) 12
White Party 53
Whitewater Preserve 79-80
WiFi 115
wildlife refuge 84
windmill tours 27

Yucca Valley 71-72

Made Easy Travel Guides to Southern California

- *Palm Springs Made Easy*: Your Guide To The Coachella Valley, Joshua Tree, Hi-Desert, Salton Sea, Idyllwild, and More!

- *San Diego Made Easy*: Sights and shopping, hotels and restaurants, day trips and nightlife in "America's Finest City"

- *The Amazing California Desert*: Your guide to Joshua Tree, Hi-Desert, Salton Sea, Palm Springs, Coachella Valley, Anza-Borrego, Death Valley, Mojave Desert, and More!

- *Southern California Made Easy*: The Top Sights of Santa Barbara, Los Angeles, San Diego, Palm Springs, Joshua Tree, Mojave Desert, Death Valley, and More!

For a list of all Made Easy travel guides, and to purchase our books, visit

Printed in Great Britain
by Amazon